HOW TO
GROW AND
USE HERBS

HOW TO
GROW AND
USE HERBS

ANN BONAR AND
DAPHNE MacCARTHY

WARD LOCK LIMITED · LONDON

ACKNOWLEDGEMENTS

The publishers gratefully acknowledge the following agencies for granting permission to reproduce the colour photographs: Mushroom Growers' Association (pp 62 and 67 (left)); Seafish Industry Authority (pp 67 (right) and 67 (top)); Meat and Livestock Commission (p. 71 (top and bottom)); British Chicken Information Service (p. 74 (top)); and British Farm Produce Council (p. 74 (bottom)). All the remaining photographs, including the cover picture, were taken by Bob Challinor.

© Ward Lock Limited 1987

First published in Great Britain in 1987
by Ward Lock Limited, 8 Clifford Street,
London W1X 1RB
An Egmont Company

House editor Denis Ingram

Text filmset in Bembo by
Paul Hicks Limited
Middleton, Manchester

Printed in Portugal

British Library Cataloguing in Publication Data
Bonar, Ann
How to grow and use herbs. – 2nd ed.
1. Cookery (Herbs)
I. Title II.   MacCarthy, Daphne
641.6'57   TX819.H4
ISBN 0–7063–6510–0

Frontispiece: Contrasting foliage colours between santolina (*centre*) and winter savory make this very simple bed effective at Hatfield House.

CONTENTS

Chapter 1

Herbs in the Garden

What is a herb? Most people regard a herb as a special type of plant, part of which is used in cooking to add another flavour or help emphasise one already there. However, when you begin to think about it, the word can cover a very wide range of plants – one could say that all herbaceous plants are herbs. The dictionary of botanical definition of a herb is: 'any plant with a soft or succulent stem or stems that dies to the roots every year', but in general any herbaceous or woody plant which is aromatic in one or more of its parts and which is considered to have culinary, medicinal or cosmetic value, can be regarded as a herb.

Herbs can be classified in a variety of different ways and any one or more of these can be pursued if the herb virus gets a hold of you. You can devote yourself to making as complete a collection as possible of the herbs used in cooking. Suggested kinds to start with are the big five: parsley, mint, thyme, chives and sage; from these you can expand to include marjoram, garlic, fennel, rosemary, sorrel, tarragon, angelica and the savories. From there you can go on to the herbs used in making teas, wines and drinks in general – there is no end to the ways in which the cook can make use of herbs.

You could concentrate on the medicinal kinds, though if you want to use them for curing ailments of various kinds, be extremely careful in consulting reliable literature, and make sure that you are sure that you are using the right plants. The plant family *Umbelliferae* contains several herbs, which are rather alike in general appearance, including hemlock which of course provides a deadly poison! It is interesting, though, to discover the old plants that were once much used by doctors; some were useless but many were effective, and the foxglove for instance is still grown to provide digitalin for use in heart complaints. The autumn crocus (*Colchicum*), comfrey, betony, aconitum, poppy and belladonna are also all considered to be medicinal herbs.

Some people prefer to collect plants in botanical groups, and herbs lend themselves rather well to this; for instance to take the family *Umbelliferae* again, it contains a good many useful herbs such as lovage, fennel, coriander, and dill, and the *Labiatae* is another, with basil, balm, hyssop and marjoram counted among its members. Each family can have a bed devoted to it, and it is easy then, and rather surprising, to see how widely plants can differ within a family in habit, shape of leaf and even apparently in flower, though a trained botanist will be able to pinpoint the similarities on which the classification is based. Collections of this kind can be seen at Kew, Cambridge and the Chelsea Physic Garden in London – the last mentioned is open to the public on certain days of the week only.

Another way of collecting herbs is to grow only those which are pleasantly aromatic or perfumed; this would of course mean no parsley, no garlic, no savory and so on, but it does leave room for quite a lot more plants, such as lavender, thyme, lemon balm, basil and mint. Some need bruising before releasing their fragrance, and growing them on paths or at the edges of beds close to paths, will ensure the necessary pressure.

One of the nicest and most satisfying ways to grow herbs is to collect them together into a small garden within a garden. It is much easier,

Gravel paths give all-weather access to the plants. Wooden surrounds to the beds ensure they remain well-defined: they also help to keep invasive herbs in their place.

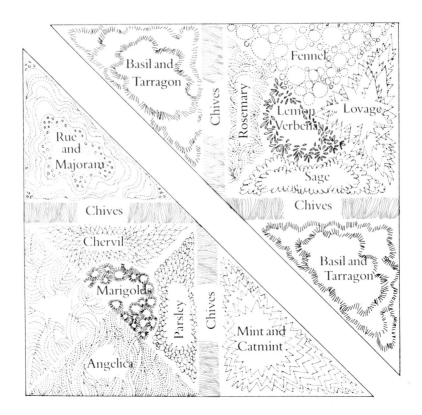

Fig. 1 A herb garden designed in a square shape.

then, to give them the special attention and conditions that they like. Most of them prefer sun and shelter from wind, and the kind of soil vegetables do best in. Paving seems to lend itself to herbs, as it gives definition to their sometimes rather untidy growth, and it can be used in a kind of chess board pattern or laid out like the spokes of a wheel. The carpeting herbs can take the place of paving, such as creeping thyme or chamomile, if paving is unobtainable.

Hedges round the herb garden will help to shelter it, or climbers trained up trellis work or similar supports; the hedges can be of herbs themselves such as lavender, rosemary, sage, sweet bay (slow to grow) or *Rosa gallica officinalis*, the Apothecaries' rose. If the garden is to be laid out in a square it could have a bed in each corner, with a centre such as a pool, sundial, or bird bath. A seat in the centre or to one side will always be popular, so that the fragrance and aroma of the herbs can be enjoyed; there is a certain old world peacefulness about a herb garden, too, which is best absorbed by lingering. If you have cats, they will nearly always be found in it somewhere peacefully asleep, knowing that they are least likely to be disturbed there. Beware, however, if you plant nepeta (catmint) – the peace will not be quite so absolute, as the cats tear it to pieces in their attempts to become one with it.

However you decide to lay out your herb garden (Figs. 1 and 2), try to design it on paper beforehand. Then you can be sure of blending the colours of foliage and flowers, and avoid the mistake of planting tall herbs in front of the mound-forming kinds. Some herbs have beautifully coloured leaves; others have an architectural habit of growth with handsomely shaped leaves; some die down completely in winter, others have attractive flowers, and all this should be taken into account when designing a herb garden. One needs to know, too, the amount of space a plant will take up in girth as well as height. Make sure that herbs which like the same conditions of growth all grow together.

An even more elaborate form of herb garden is one laid out as the Elizabethan knot gardens used to be. These consisted of intricate arrangements of small beds separated by low growing hedges, or paths of coloured stones or sand. Box *(Buxus suffruticosa* 'Sempervirens') makes a good low dividing hedge, though not considered a true herb; others are santolina (lavender cotton), sage or artemisia. There is a

Fig. 2 A herb garden made in an old cart wheel.

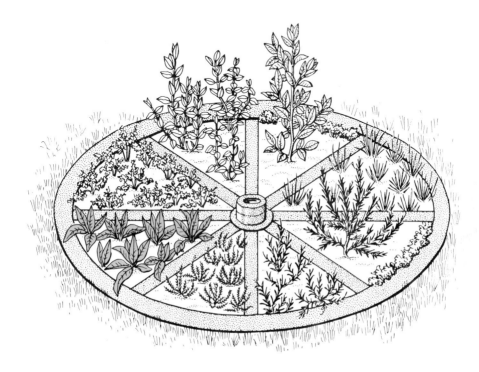

typical Elizabethan knot garden laid out at Hampton Court, and another at New Place, Stratford-upon-Avon.

For those who would like the effect of a lawn in a herb garden, a good substitute for grass is chamomile, which will stand a certain amount of walking on, and will not need much cutting, perhaps three or four times during spring and summer. It makes a good green carpet, as do also creeping thyme, the creeping form of pennyroyal and the creeping mint *Mentha requienii*. Paths within the herb garden can be covered with these plants as an alternative to paving or bricks; walking on them will help to release their aromatic perfumes, as the leaves and stems are bruised by the pressure.

Readers wishing to visit herb gardens open to the public, which will give them an idea of what can be achieved, are advised to contact The Herb Society, 77 Great Peter Street, London SW1.

Besides growing herbs in their own garden, they can be given a separate border, like a herbaccous border. The same principles of design will apply to this as to the herbaceous kind, in that tall plants are better at the back, and plants should be grown closely enough to prevent weeds establishing themselves. Good front-of-border plants are things like the golden-leaved marjoram, chives, parsley and thyme. The rounded, busy, middle-of-the-border plants are hyssop, sorrel, lemon balm, pot marjoram, tarragon and vervain, and for giving height and architectural quality, angelica, fennel, and lovage can be used. Facing the sun, and with a tall hedge as backing, a herb border can look very ornamental as well as being useful, particularly if some of the medicinal herbs are included, such as foxglove, lily of the valley and poppies whose flowers are more showy than those of the purely culinary herbs.

Since the majority of herbs are grown for cooking, another good site would seem to be the vegetable garden, giving them a permanent small border to themselves, alongside the vegetables. The perennial herbs will obviously stay in the same place for some years, but those which are annual and are grown afresh from seed every year will need freshly prepared soil each year, and therefore require a little more time and attention.

Still, this can be done at the same time as the ground is prepared for vegetable sowing. Herb seeds are sown in drills, and thinned, as vegetables are, and will need hoeing to remove weeds, and watering in dry weather, with occasional applications of liquid fertilisers. Try to make sure that a part of the vegetable garden is chosen which supplies the conditions of sun, shelter, and well-drained soil mentioned previously.

Obviously, one of the best places to grow cooking herbs is as near the kitchen as possible. There is nothing more irritating than getting halfway through a recipe and discovering that you have forgotten to pick the particular herbs needed for it, and then having to go to the end of the garden for them. It is always a dark night, pouring with rain, when this happens, and it is terribly tempting, then, to do without. At least if they are just outside the backdoor, they are quick to get if you have forgotten to pick in advance.

An even more convenient way to grow just a few different kinds of herbs is in the form of 'mobile' herbs, that is in window boxes, pots, hanging baskets and miniature gardens. They can then be moved about and given the best possible position for light and sun. Soil mixtures, feeding and watering can be tailored to fit their requirements exactly, and it ensures that garden-less cooks can not only have their own home grown herbs, but can also have them at any time. Quite a few herbs which will not survive our winters out of doors can be retained all the year round in this way. Balconies, outer window sills and roof gardens can be pressed into use; inside window ledges which get plenty of light are excellent.

A pleasing pattern need not be complex, as this small formal garden at Clack's Farm shows.

CHAPTER 2

HERBS AND THEIR CULTIVATION

The joy about herb gardening is that it is easy. Herbs are not faddy plants which demand, for instance, such niceties as acid soil, regular feeding, a lot of manure, shade at midday, mulching with oak leaves, and so on. They do like shelter from wind but what plant, or person for that matter, does not like protection from all the gales that blow? Given a reasonable average soil, they should all grow perfectly well, and indeed often the trouble is, as with vegetables, they produce far more vegetation than one can comfortably use. Still, if they are being grown mainly for ornament, even this will not matter.

Probably most important of all is to choose the right position in the garden. Somewhere facing south and/or west, with a barrier against the north-east winds, and some kind of screen to break the force of the south-west gales of summer, will make a very good site for herbs. If the ground slopes a little towards the sun, it is even better, but this is not so important. Try to avoid a part of the garden which tends to remain frozen long after other parts have thawed; many herbs are natives of the hills and coasts of the Mediterranean and are used to baking heat in summer and dry winters with little if any frost. Actually, it is not so much low temperatures, as the alternation of cold and warmth in winter combined with constant damp which we get in Britain, that is responsible for killing plants.

If there is a suitably sunny position, but no barriers to wind, a temporary screen of hessian or wattle fencing will provide this, while a hedge grows up. Even trellis work or strands of wire will be effective, if climbing plants such as sweet peas, nasturtiums, runner beans or ornamental hops are grown over them.

The hedge can be formal or informal, tall to give a completely enclosed garden, or low growing, in the pattern of the Elizabethan knot garden. The plants forming the hedge need not be herbs, though there are some very good ones for this, for instance, rosemary, *Rosa gallica*, and sage.

Soil which becomes sodden in winter or after prolonged rain must have its ability to drain water away improved. This can be done by forking in coarse sand at 1½–2 kg (3–4 lb) per sq yd while preparing the soil. Peat will help the soil particles to form into crumbs, and so help to make room for air and water to circulate. It can be mixed in at the rates the suppliers suggest; leafmould at 3 kg (7 lb) per sq yd, or rotted garden compost at a lower rate because it contains more plant food. For heavy soils these preparations can be made during the late autumn or early winter. Soil which is already quick to dry out will only need the addition of organic matter, a month or so before sowing or planting. If mixed into such a soil earlier, it is in fact liable to be washed out by the winter rains.

If the soil is really short of plant food, as town garden or old garden soils often are, you must give some kind of artificial fertiliser before sowing or planting. Herbs are said not to require a particularly fertile soil, but it is no good expecting them to do well if the growing medium is dead, that is, if there is neither mineral nutrient nor humus in it.

Some people will say that artificial fertilisers should never be used, but in some soils plants will never get going without them no matter how much humus is put in. Once the soil fertility has been built up and the soil brought to life again, by feeding and manuring and regular cultivation, then it may be possible to do without powder and granulated fertilisers, and rely completely on a little mulching (spreading a surface layer) with compost, leafmould, or peat.

In short, preparation of the soil before planting herbs should consist either of adding coarse sand and peat/leafmould/compost or similar material if drainage is bad, in late autumn, or it should consist of mixing in organic matter about a month before planting or sowing. In both cases fertilizer can be given ten days or so before sowing or planting at 70–80 g (2–3 oz) per sq yd, raking it into the top 5 or 8 cm (2 or 3 in) or so.

A word about compost making here. Compost heaps first came on the scene when a shortage of farm manure began to be apparent, as horse-drawn ploughs were replaced by tractors and as towns became bigger and more distant from sources of supply. Whereas farm manure is mainly animal organic matter, compost is mainly vegetable in origin, containing rotted down leaves, soft stems, flowers, grass cuttings, in fact all kinds of soft vegetation; household refuse can also be included such as tea leaves, orange skins, potato peelings and so on. The ideal size of the heap is about 1.5 × 1.2 × 1.5 m (5 × 4 × 5 ft).

Such a heap heats up rapidly and to a considerable temperature if built quickly, using the above materials, with the addition of a sprinkling of lime alternating with a sprinkling of nitrogenous fertiliser on every 15 cm (6 in) layer of vegetation. A very wet or dry heap will not rot, and adjustments must be made to either condition.

A heap started in spring should be ready for use about six to eight weeks after completion; one started in mid-summer probably will take all the winter to rot down completely to a dark brown crumbly substance. Complete rotting of the heap will be assisted if it can be raised off the ground slightly so that there is air beneath it, which will be drawn up through the centre. If the heap is built up round posts, their removal when the heap is finished will improve ventilation even more. Wooden slats will help to keep the heap tidy; for small gardens plastic bins can be obtained, some of which are easily dismantled and packed flat when not wanted.

The benefit to the ground which results from using compost material made in this way is out of all proportion to the quantities added. The bacteria and worms contained in it continue to live, feed and work not only in the compost but in the soil also, water and air become much more mobile, particles of plant food dissolve in the soil moisture much more readily, so there is more nutrient for roots to absorb, and so on and so on. The end product of compost-treated soils cannot help but be better herbs in all respects, whether healthier, stronger, larger, more aromatic or with increased food and medicinal value.

As with other garden plants, herbs can be annuals or perennials. The annuals are grown from seed and will flower, if allowed to, and die down in one growing season, between spring and autumn; the perennials will grow from seed or small plants obtained from cuttings or division. Some of the perennials will also die down in autumn so that only the rootstock remains, but some are evergreen, and the leaves can be used all through the winter. Those that grow conveniently like this are: chervil, parsley, rosemary, thyme, sage, lavender, bay and winter savory; some other herbs can be encouraged to go on producing top growth into early winter if covered with cloches, or through the winter if potted and brought indoors, such as chives, hyssop, mints, lemon balm, pot marjoram, salad burnet and lemon verbena. Some of the shrubs may not survive a severe winter – for instance lavender, rosemary, sage, bay and hyssop, and if it looks like being prolonged and chilly, they must be protected from the cold as far as possible. A thick, wide-spreading mulch will help the roots, and enclosing the top growth in straw or conifer branches wrapped round with polythene, securely tied against wind, will keep the worst of the cold out. Leave a space at the top for a little air to penetrate and remove the wrappings as soon as it is safe to do so.

On the whole, about two thirds of the commonly grown herbs do die completely or to ground level in autumn, and so for some at any rate, one must resort to preservation in order to use them between

Herb beds need not be straight borders—an island bed is often more practical and effective.

mid-autumn and mid-spring. With modern methods, such as green drying, or deep freezing, the flavour and aroma can be retained almost *in toto*, and lack of fresh material need not be a deterrent to herb cookery, or any other uses to which they may be put. Most herb seeds are sown in spring in early or mid-spring, depending on the weather and the area. There can be a difference of four or five weeks between sowing dates, according to the air temperature and the rate at which the soil in your garden warms up, and it is much better to sow later than to rush the seeds into the ground, only to have them rot in cold, wet soil.

In any case, waterlogged soil cannot be broken down to the fine tilth required for seed sowing; it needs to be almost breadcrumb structure. Digging, knocking down the lumps with the back of the rake, and then repeatedly raking will gradually reduce it to the fine state in which seeds will germinate and the seedlings can establish and grow. Take out the weeds at the same time, particularly the roots of the perennial kinds, such as bindweed and couch grass; also remove debris such as stones, sticks, glass, pieces of clay pot, marbles, tin cans, and all the other clutter that is likely to be found in the average garden soil.

In the border or vegetable garden, herb seeds are most conveniently grown if the seeds are sown in rows or drills, as vegetables are, drawing out a shallow drill 1–1.5 cm (¼–½ in) deep depending on the size of the seed. As the seedlings will, in most cases, need thinning later, it pays to sow the seeds sparingly. Choose a calm day, when the soil is nicely moist, give it a final rake down, and cover the seed thinly. If the soil structure is not good, germination can be encouraged by lining the drills´with one of the soilless seed composts, suitably moistened.

Some herbs are grown from rooted cuttings, particularly the shrubby ones, and these are taken generally in summer, using soft tip or semi-ripe shoots. The majority which are propagated in this way root easily and it does not take long to increase or replace one's stock. The tip cuttings, about 8 cm (3 in) long, are put round the edges of 8 cm (3 in) pots, in one of the proprietary cutting composts, covered with a polythene bag secured with a rubber band, and put in a warm shady place until they begin to lengthen. When this happens, they have rooted, and may be potted on separately. Semi-ripe cuttings 13–15 cm (5 or 6 in) long are taken later in the summer and need only be put, in their pots, in a cold frame or under a cloche out of doors. They will take longer to root and are usually best planted out in a nursery bed in the spring following rooting.

Some herbs can also be propagated by division in spring or autumn, as herbaceous perennials are.

Whatever method of increase is chosen, once the young plants have settled down and are growing well, the routine cultivation through the season need only consist of thinning the seedlings, hoeing or hand weeding, watering when the weather is very dry, and perhaps giving the occasional liquid feed. Don't overdo the feeding, however; in many soils it will not be necessary, and too much tends to make herbs less aromatic and less well flavoured. They become soft and leafy, and it is the harder grown kinds that contain the most in the way of essential oils, nutrients and minerals.

Where the appearance of the herbs is important, for instance in a herb garden or border, or when they are grown mixed with other plants, some will need trimming and cutting back, to keep them tidy. They can look very straggly when they have finished flowering, and get blown about and flattened by the wind. The small shrubby herbs tend to get unkempt unless sheared back occasionally.

Fortunately troubles such as insect pests and fungus diseases are few and far between as far as herbs are concerned; it has been said that they carry their own built-in resistance to such invasions, which is perhaps why they have such considerable medicinal values. Such pests and diseases as they do get are specific to the herb concerned and will be mentioned in the individual description in the alphabetical list, together with the remedy.

CONTAINER GROWN HERBS

Two points are particularly important for growing herbs in this way: good compost and good light. As with any pot or box grown plant, good compost is essential, that is, one which is well drained, and to which not only has plant food been added but in the right proportions. The John Innes compost No 1 is suitable containing, as it does, 7 parts by bulk good loam, 3 parts peat and 2 parts coarse sand, together with 0.2 kg (4 oz) of the J.I. base fertilizer and 25 g (¾ oz) chalk to each bushel of the mixture. No 2 and No 3 have twice as much and three times as much respectively of the base fertilizer and chalk. These composts can be bought ready made up, from chain stores and garden shops.

Sunlight is most important, so herbs should be put in a sunny position if possible, whether outside on a windowsill or balcony, or indoors on a window ledge. If out of doors, try to find somewhere that is not plagued by wind and if inside, give them even temperatures and a humid atmosphere as far as possible.

Herbs seem to do best if grown in the larger containers, such as window boxes, troughs, and shallow tubs. They can also be grown in pots; the 10 cm (4 in) size is the smallest that can be satisfactorily used for the majority of herbs. When planting in clay pots, put a little drainage material at the bottom of the pot, such as crocks (pieces of broken clay pot) with the curved side uppermost, and then fill in with compost to about half full. Sit the plant on top of this in the centre of the pot, and fill in with compost round it, firming it down with the fingers and leaving 1.5 cm (½ in) space at the top for watering; water in lightly to settle the plant into the compost. Re-potting, or potting on into larger pots, is usually done in spring.

Whatever else you do when watering container-grown herbs, don't give them a dribble every day. Give them a good watering which fills the space between the compost surface and the rim of the container, let any extra water drain through the drainage hole, and then leave the plant alone until the surface soil begins to dry; when this happens, it usually becomes lighter in colour. A dry pot is lighter in weight then a moist one and, if it is clay, it will produce a ringing tone when tapped with a wooden stick. The rule is: only water when the plant needs it as indicated by these signs, and not, for example, at 10.30 every Thursday morning, or every day as soon as the breakfast washing up is done. Herbs will probably die more quickly from overwatering than any other container-grown plant, so, if you must err, do so on the dry side. Remember, too, that in winter when they are virtually not growing, much less water is needed than in summer.

CHAPTER 3

HERBS—
A DESCRIPTIVE LIST

Angelica (*Angelica archangelica; Umbelliferae*)
Description A tall, stout plant 2–3 × 1 m (5–8 × 3 ft), perennial if prevented from flowering, otherwise biennial. Large, dark green leaves divided into leaflets, and flat, spreading heads of creamy white flowers in mid-summer. Origin, Northern Hemisphere, introduced 1568.

Uses Young green stems and leaf stalks used for candying for cakes and dessert decoration, picked mid-late spring. Leaves also sometimes used in cooking. Plant strongly flavoured in all its parts, reminiscent of juniper berries, said to be used in making the French liqueur Chartreuse. Roots recommended for medicinal use as a digestive and for blood cleansing.

History Said to be named after the Archangel Michael who brought the curative properties of the plant to the notice of a monk. It was once recommended for use against the Plague, and to ward off the evil eye, spells and wizardry in general.

Cultivation Put in small plants in spring and divide roots when established; seeds will distribute themselves in due course. If using seed, sow as soon as ripe in late summer, as viability lost very quickly, thin out when large enough to handle, or plant in permanent positions in autumn, about 45 cm (1½ ft) apart. Moist soil and semi-shady place preferred.

Balm, lemon (*Melissa officinalis; Labiatae*)
Description A hardy herbaceous perennial 60–100 × 45 cm (2–3 × 1½ ft), rather shrub-like in form. Leaves are soft, heart-shaped and wrinkled (Fig. 3); whitish flowes are produced early to late summer. Origin, Europe, naturalised in Britain; used since the Middle Ages. Top growth dies to ground in winter, but new shoots appear very early in spring.

Uses The strongly lemon scented leaves are used in drinks, also in

An informal border filled with strong-growing plants; tall tansy and rosemary at the back, brightly variegated ginger mint in the centre.

salads, sauces and omelettes. It is said to be useful for indigestion and to relieve tension. A favourite plant for pot pourri and perfumery, and is a plant liked by bees because the flowers contain much nectar.

History Used by the Greeks – *melissa* is the Greek word for honey bee. It was also used by the Romans, and in the days of the Tudors leaves were strewn on the floors, and the oil was an ingredient of furniture polish. In the 18th century it was popular enough to warrant growing on a commercial scale in market gardens round London.

Cultivation Easily grown by division of established plants in autumn, or from seeds sown in spring in a frame. Germination takes 3–4 weeks, and young plants are put out in early autumn. Will grow in most soils and situations, but does best in sun and moist, well drained soil. Remove flowers to encourage leaf production.

Basil, sweet (*Ocimum basilicum, Labiatae*)
Description Half hardy annual, 60–90 × 30 cm (2–3 × 1 ft); light green, thin leaves up to 7 cm (3 in) long (Fig. 3); white flowers in late summer. Purple basil, a variety of this, has deep purple leaves and violet-coloured flowers, also in spikes, making it highly ornamental as well as useful. Origin, tropical Asia, Africa and the Pacific Islands.

Fig. 3 Sweet Basil

Fig. 4 Sweet Bay

Uses Leaves strongly and sweetly aromatic, similar to clove, used in cookery, particularly in Italy, and in India for curries. Because of its powerful flavour, sparing use should be made of it. The oil is used in perfume, and medicinally it is particularly of help in curing headaches and migraines.

History Has had a chequered history, being loved and hated almost equally. Culpeper (1616–54) said that: 'This is the herb which all authors are together by the ears about and rail at one another like lawyers'. Ocimum is from *okimon*, a name used for the plant in ancient Greece; basilicum is from the Latin *basilica,* princely or royal.

Cultivation Sow seed in 13–16° C (55–60° F) in mid-spring; germination will take about a fortnight. Prick out, harden off and plant indoors in late spring 20 cm (9 in) apart, in sandy rich soil and a sunny position. Seedlings transplant badly, so either sow generously inside or sow outdoors in late spring, and thin later. Water freely in dry weather; pinch out the tops for bushiness. Lift in early autumn and pot up, for early winter use, cutting back the top growth hard.

Bay, sweet (*Laurus nobilis; Lauraceae*)

Description A large, evergreen shrub or tree, not hardy in severe cold (Fig. 4); can form a tree 6 m (20 ft) tall in southern England. Insignificant pale yellow flowers in late spring, followed by black berries in hot summers. Origin, Southern Europe.

Uses Leaves strongly flavoured and much used in cooking, alone or as part of a bouquet garni. Berries and leaves much used formerly for medicinal purposes.

History Used to make wreaths in Roman times to honour poets, (hence the term poet laureate), generals, athletes and students, particularly medical students. Culpeper considered that it 'resisteth witchcraft very potently', and advised that 'the berries are very effectual against the sting of wasps and bees'. The diarist John Evelyn recommended its use against ague. For many years it was used with other evergreens for decorations at Christmas.

Cultivation Any soil and a sunny, sheltered place suit it. Young plants are put in during autumn or spring; heel cuttings can be taken in early summer, or 7–10 cm (3–4 in) half-ripe cuttings in late summer in a cold frame, in pots, potting-on as required. Plant out next autumn in nursery bed for two years. Layer lowest shoots in late summer/early autumn. Clip trained plants twice in mid-summer and early autumn. A good container plant as pyramid or standard.

Bergamot (*Monarda didyma; Labiatae*)

Description A hardy perennial often grown in the herbaceous border, which dies down to the crown each autumn (Fig. 5). Height 30–60 cm (1–2 ft), spread 30 cm (1 ft). Heads of tubular bright red flowers appear early to late summer. Origin, eastern America, introduced 1656. Also called Oswego Tea, or Bee Balm.

Uses The orange-scented leaves are mainly used for making tea, and on the Continent as a sleep-inducing tisane. In addition, they can be added to other drinks, chopped up for salads and occasionally used in pot pourri.

History Named after Nicolas Monardez, a Spanish botanist of the 16th century. Used by American colonists as a substitute for British tea during the time of the Boston Tea Party, and called Oswego tea after the American Indians from Lake Ontario who also used it for tea.

Fig. 5 Bergamot   **Fig. 6** Borage

Cultivation Monarda prefers damp soil and does well at the waterside in sunny, open or semi-shady places. Plant in autumn or spring, mulch with compost each year at these times also. Cut back in autumn to tidy. Increase by dividing in spring.

Borage (*Borago officinalis; Boraginaceae*)
Description A hardy annual to 90 cm (3 ft) tall and 45 cm (1½ ft) wide, with large leaves to 22 cm (9 in) long, rough and hairy, and brilliant blue flowers in drooping clusters from early summer to early autumn (Fig. 6). Origin uncertain – it may be a native plant, or it may be naturalised as a garden escape. It has been widely grown here in Britain, however, at least since Elizabethan times.

Uses The cucumber-like flavour that the fresh leaves and flowers give to drinks or salads is very refreshing; the flowers are used to give colour to pot pourri, or candied for cake decoration. It was once used medicinally for inflammations and redness of the eyes.

History It is possible that borage was introduced by the Crusaders; borage is said to be the herb of courage from the days of ancient Greece. Borage comes from the Latin *borra* meaning rough hair – the whole plant is bristly. It was widely grown in the past as a salad plant.

Cultivation Sow seed outdoors in early autumn or mid-spring, thinning to 30 cm (12 in) apart in ordinary soil. Flowering will start in

Tansy (*Tanacetum vulgare*) has attractive finely cut foliage and yellow button flowers, but is very invasive.

late spring, or early to mid-summer, depending on time of sowing. For winter cultivation indoors, sow seeds in containers in early autumn. Flowering may continue through a mild winter.

Caraway (*Carum carvi; Umbelliferae*)

Description A taprooted, hardy biennial to 60 cm (2 ft) tall, with frond-like, much divided leaves, and umbels of small white flowers in early summer the second year after sowing seed. Origin, Europe to India, cultivated in Britain for many centuries, possibly since the time of the Romans.

Uses The small, black, narrow seeds are the seed of the seedcake, or caraway cake; they are also used in biscuits, bread and cheese, in fact in very many dishes and receipes. Young roots can be used as a vegetable rather like parsnip or carrot, and the leaves in salads. Oil from the seeds is used to perfume Brown Windsor soup, and some Continental liqueurs, for instance Kummel.

History Caraway was prescribed by Culpeper for flatulence, and the powder of the seeds put into a poultice would take away the 'Black and blue spots of blows and bruises'. It was described in an Egyptian papyrus in 2,500 B.C. and was also used medicinally by the Greeks and Romans. Seedcakes were popular in Tudor and Elizabethan days.

Cultivation Seeds are sown outdoors in spring in rows 30 cm (1 ft) apart, thinning to the same distance. Supply a well drained soil and sunny place – winter waterlogging will kill it. Harvest the seeds in mid to late summer the following year.

Chamomile (*Chamaemelum nobile, Anthemis nobilis; Compositae*)

Description Roman chamomile is a low growing herbaceous perennial 15–22 cm (6–9 in) tall, spreading to about 30 cm (1 ft). Leaves very finely cut and fern-like, forming a thick covering; white daisy flowers about 2½ cm (1 in) wide from early to late summer. There is a non-flowering strain called the Treneague strain. It remains green through the winter. Origin: a native plant. There is also *Matricaria chamomilla*, wild chamomile, also a native plant, very similar in appearance, but taller, to about 40 cm (15 in); this is an annual.

Uses Roman chamomile is used mainly for small lawns; it has some medicinal properties. Wild chamomile flowers are used considerably in medicine, and for shampoos. A tisane made of the flowers helps in

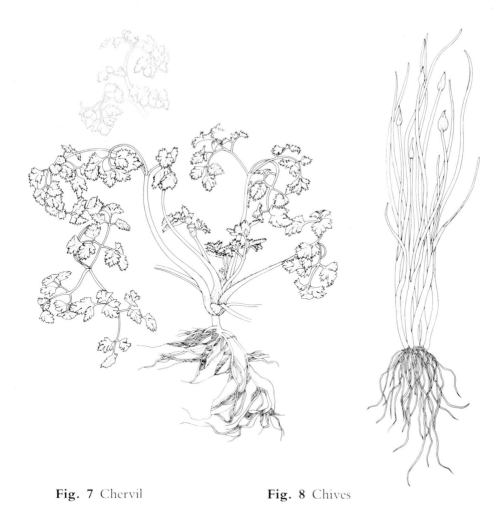

Fig. 7 Chervil   **Fig. 8** Chives

digestion and is popular on the Continent, and a concentrated infusion acts as an emetic. All parts of the plant are strongly aromatic.

History Roman chamomile has been used for hundreds of years to make lawns; it was probably used for the lawn on which Drake was playing bowls when the Armada hove in sight. A chamomile of some kind is said to have been used by the ancient Egyptians, and it was certainly much used by the Greeks and Romans.

Cultivation Roman chamomile can be grown from rooted cuttings put out in spring in a sandy soil and sunny place about 15 cm (6 in) apart for a lawn, or about 30 cm (12 in) apart, if grown as a herb. Chamomile lawns are cut three or four times a year. Seed is sown in spring outdoors and later thinned, or indoors under glass in late winter.

The soft colour of purple sage contrasts well with variegated ginger mint. In the background is a steel–blue rue and the pale pink flowers of chives.

Angelica archangelica: a statuesque herb whose leaves and stems are both used as flavouring.

Chervil (*Anthriscus cerefolium; Umbelliferae*)

Description A hardy biennial usually grown as an annual with delicate much cut and lacy leaves, flowering stems to 45 cm (1½ ft) and small white flowers in clusters from early to late summer in the second year from sowing (Fig. 7). Origin, south-eastern Europe, naturalised in some places.

Uses Leaves have a slightly peppery and parsley-like flavour and are the part used, mainly for cooking, in sauces, soup and salads and in particular in omelette fines herbes. Chervil has a medicinal value in cleansing the blood and clearing skin troubles.

History Introduced by the Romans to this country, it continued to be used from Anglo-Saxon times continuously till late in the last century. Though little used now in this country, it is still very much part of modern French cooking. First used medicinally, and being considered an essential member of the herb garden in Elizabeth I's day, the flavour was later found to be palatable, and it became popular for cooking.

Cultivation Sow seed outdoors in succession at four-week intervals from late winter to mid-autumn in a well drained soil, in drills, thinning to 30 cm (1 ft) apart. It does not like drying out. Cut the leaves about 6–8 weeks after sowing, and a further crop will be produced. A late summer sowing will give leaves in early to mid-autumn and early spring, or earlier if protected by cloches. Window boxes and pots are also suitable for overwintering. The seed loses its viability quickly.

Chives (*Allium schoenoprasum; Alliaceae*)

Description Perennial bulbous plants with tubular, grasslike leaves to 10–25 cm (4–10 in), which die down to ground level in late autumn (Fig. 8). Round heads of purple flowers in early to mid-summer. There is a giant variety, to 45 cm (1½ ft) tall, much less well-flavoured. Origin, the Northern Hemisphere but rarely found naturally in Britain.

Uses Almost exclusively in cooking, for the delicate onion flavour of the leaves. Seldom used medicinally, though they are said to have some slight good effect on digestion.

History The cultivation of chives dates back to their use in 3000 B.C. by the Chinese and they have been used ever since by various civilisations. Introduced to this country by the Romans, the word *schoenoprasum* gives the plant its other, ancient common name of rush leek, since *schoenos* is a rush and *prason*, a leek, both being derived from Greek.

Cultivation Sow seeds outdoors in spring 25 cm (10 in) apart in drills in medium to heavy soil and sun or shade; thin to clumps about 15 cm (6 in) apart. Also increase by dividing in spring or autumn. Remove the flowers to encourage leaf production; water well in dry weather. Mulch in autumn with garden compost. Cover with cloches to protect from frost as long as possible, or pot up and grow on an indoor window sill in 15 cm (6 in) pots.

Coriander (*Coriandrum sativum; Umbelliferae*)
Description A hardy annual 45 × 20 cm (18 × 8 in) with delicate deeply cut, stem leaves; the base leaves are more solidly lobed. Both types have an unpleasant strong smell. Tiny white flowers, tinted violet, are produced in flat heads in early to mid-summer. The round seeds are ripe in late summer. Origin: southern Europe, naturalised in Britain.

Uses The seeds are the part which is used most; they have a strong and unpleasant odour when unripe, but the disappearance of this indicates their ripeness; in fact their fragrance improves with age. The flavour is a mixture of orange and sage. Powder of the seeds is much used in cooking, for instance curry, drinks including liqueurs and in both meat and dessert dishes of Spain, Greece, the Middle East and India.

History The name *coriandrum* comes from the Greek *koris*, meaning a bug, since the general odour was thought to be the same as that of bedbugs! Coriander seeds have been used at least since Egyptian times 1,000 years before Pliny; they are mentioned in the Bible, and there is record of their use here since 1289.

Cultivation Sow the seeds out of doors in mid-spring preferably in a warm soil, otherwise germination is slow, in rows about 30 cm (1 ft) apart, thinning to 20–23 cm (8–9 in). Also in early autumn, or under glass in early spring, to plant out in late spring. Collect the seeds in late summer when their unpleasant smell has gone.

Dill (*Anethum graveolens; Umbelliferae*)
Description A hardy annual 60–90 × 30 cm (2–3 × 1 ft), rather like

Fig. 9 Dill

fennel to look at, with ferny, very finely divided leaves, and a stout stem; small dull yellow flowers come in large clusters between early and late summer (Fig. 9). Origin, the Mediterranean countries; has been grown in Britain since the Roman occupation.

Uses Mostly culinary, in the case of the leaves, for salads, fish and vegetables; the seeds have a bitter taste but supply gripe water and are otherwise useful for digestion. The seeds are also mildly sleep inducing.

History The name comes from the old Norse word *dilla*, meaning to lull, because it was found to be effective in overcoming insomnia, and for soothing and calming generally. The ancient Egyptians used it, the Romans used it in Italy, and Culpeper in the 17th century remarked that 'It stayeth the hiccough'.

Cultivation Sow seeds outdoors in early to mid-spring in a moist but

Fig. 10 Fennel   **Fig. 11** Garlic

draining soil, in sun. Germination takes 14–21 days depending on the soil temperature. Rows should be about 30 cm (1 ft) apart; thin to 22 cm (9 in). It does not like being transplanted. Sow also in mid-summer for an autumn supply. Keep well watered to prevent premature flowering. Self sown plants will be stronger than their parents (see Fennel: cultivation).

Fennel (*Foeniculum vulgare; Umbelliferae*)
Description A tall, stout hardy perennial 150–180 cm (5–6 ft) tall by about 60 cm (2 ft) with a long white carrot-like root, rather short lived. Very finely cut, fern-like leaves, branching stems, and flat-headed

clusters of yellow flowers in mid-late summer (Fig. 10). The variety *dulce* or *azoricum* is Florence fennel or finocchio, with a bulbous rootstock. A native of southern Europe, naturalised in Britain for many centuries, particularly near southern coasts and estuaries.

Uses The leaves have a strong and unusual flavour, and are used in cooking, mostly with fish. The basal stems of Florence fennel are eaten as a vegetable. Medicinally it was thought to have weight reducing properties; the liquid is used to make a solution for bathing the eyes. It can also be used as part of a face pack.

History Another herb dating back to Pliny's day, 2,000 years ago, and beyond to the Egyptian civilisations. It is mentioned in the Anglo-Saxon poem *Piers Plowman*, the reference there obviously being to its property of preventing the feeling of hunger. Florence fennel was first grown here in 1623.

Cultivation Sow seed outdoors in mid-spring in sun or slight shade and a moist, chalky soil, in rows 45 cm (1½ ft) apart, thinning to 45–50 cm (1½–2 ft) and stake the plant as it grows. In winter, transplant into pots and keep indoors or under glass. Do not grow from seed obtained from fennel growing near dill, as the resultant plants will be hybrids, and not true fennel. These plants readily cross-pollinate.

Garlic (*Allium sativum; Alliaceae*)
Description A hardy perennial usually grown as an annual in Britain, with a bulbous base made of separate segments called cloves, and grass-like leaves about 30 cm (1 ft) tall (Fig. 11). Flower stem to 60 cm (2 ft), and flower white, appearing in summer. Origin doubtful, possibly the Kirghiz desert of Central Asia, but now grows naturally throughout the world including Britain.

Uses Has very strong flavour and odour, mostly onion-like, but with a characteristic all its own; this makes it a herb to use sparingly in cooking, where it has widespread use. Thought to have considerable antiseptic and antibiotic qualities, particularly for stomach infections and blood cleansing.

History The word garlic is a compound one, from *gar*, a spear and *leac*, a leek. The derivation is Anglo-Saxon, but it is more than likely that it was introduced here by the Romans. It is said to have been fed to the slaves who built the Egyptian pyramids, and it has been used consistently in Britain for many centuries. In mediaeval times it was held to be an ingredient of medicines to cure leprosy.

Cultivation Plant the cloves in late winter, early spring or between early and late autumn, in a light rich soil and sunny place. Distance apart about 20 cm (8 in), just below the soil surface, in rows 30 cm (1 ft) apart. Remove the flowering stems. Harvest when the leaves are yellow and hang to dry in a warm but shady place. Use a new site every year to avoid attack by white rot.

Horseradish (*Armoracia rusticana; Cruciferae*)
Description A stout perennial to 60 cm (2 ft) tall, with large basal leaves 30–60 cm (1–2 ft) long and small white flowers in late-spring (Fig. 12). The roots are fleshy and fanged. Origin, eastern Europe, naturalised in Britain, and sometimes a pernicious weed.

Fig. 12 Horseradish

Uses Now mainly used in cooking, the peppery roots being grated and used for horseradish sauce in particular. Also antibiotic qualities and a good effect on digestion. Was formerly prescribed against scurvy.

History Widely used for many centuries, particularly in Germany where it seems to have replaced mustard in the past. Its use in this country did not become general, however, until the 17th century, when it was sliced in vinegar and eaten with meat. Horseradish has been placed in a variety of genera, and was once *Cochlearia armoracia; cochlea* is the Latin for spoon, in reference to the spoon shaped leaves of some species.

Cultivation Supply a rich, moist soil worked to 60 cm (2 ft) depth. Plant 7 cm (3 in) root cutting in early spring 30 cm (1 ft) apart, just covered with soil, in a bed separate from other plants. Lift all the plants in late autumn, store the larger roots in sand for cooking, and retain the smaller, also in sand, for planting next spring. Regular new plantings thus ensure the best quality roots for cooking.

Hyssop (*Hyssopus officinalis; Labiatae*)
Description A shrub-like, hardy perennial, semi-evergreen, to 45 cm (1½ ft) × 30 cm (1 ft) wide. Pink, white or blue-violet flowers in mid-summer. Leaves narrow, like rosemary, but much less leathery (Fig. 13). Origin, Mediterranean area and east to Central Asia, date of introduction to Britain not definite.

Uses The aromatic leaves have a mint-like odour, and are slightly bitter and peppery, so use in cooking should be sparing. Hyssop is used in Chartreuse liqueur. Medicinally hyssop tea has some use for catarrh and for clearing up bruises, and further use is in perfume, especially eau-de-cologne.

History Thought to have been brought to Britain by the Romans, it was one of the herbs in a list made out by the Abbot of Cirencester in the 12th century; it is in some old Saxon manuscripts. Edgings to Elizabethan knot gardens were often of hyssop. Culpeper considered it 'an excellent medicine for the quinsy, or swelling in the throat'.

Cultivation Sow seeds in mid-spring outdoors, thinning to 30 cm (1 ft) apart in rows 45 cm (1½ ft) apart. Take 5 cm (2 in) cuttings in mid-late spring in peat/sand, and put in a cold frame. Pot up when

Fig. 13 Hyssop

rooted and plant out in autumn. Bought-in plants are planted in autumn or spring. A heavy, wet soil and a cold winter are likely to kill it.

Lemon-scented verbena (*Lippia citriodora; Verbenaceae*)
Description A tender, shrubby plant, to 120 cm (4 ft), although 3–5 m (10–15 ft) in its native Chile. Hardy in the West country outdoors. Shining, long-pointed, narrow leaves with lilac flowers in fluffy clusters in late summer (Fig. 14). Introduced 1784.

Uses Strongly lemon flavoured leaves used in cooking and for tea, much drunk in Spain. Helps to ease troubles in the respiratory tract, as well as being pleasantly flavoured. Also added to pot-pourri.

Melissa officinalis aureus: golden variegated balm. This easily grown plant adds a splash of bright colour to the herb garden. The leaves have a distinct lemon scent and flavour.

History Formerly known as *Aloysia citriodora*, it is often confused with vervain, *Verbena officinalis*, also called verbena. This is a totally different plant with a slightly bitter flavour, native to this country and considered a sacred plant by the Druids. The roots were recommended to be worn as a charm for use against scrofula, as late as 1837.

Cultivation Grow from tip cuttings taken in spring, rooted under glass in warmth. Pot on as required and, after hardening off, plant out in late spring to early summer in a sunny sheltered place and dryish, rather poor soil. Mulch heavily for winter, or lift and pot up in autumn for indoor growth, cutting it back by about half.

Lovage (*Levisticum officinale; Umbelliferae*)
Description A perennial with stout, hollow stems to 2 m (6 ft) tall; it has fleshy roots and toothed leaves divided into leaflets like celeriac

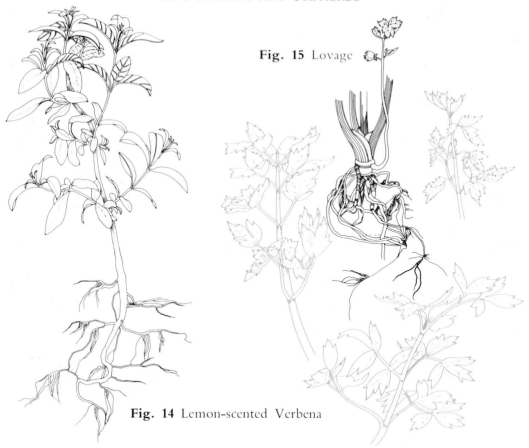

Fig. 15 Lovage

Fig. 14 Lemon-scented Verbena

(Fig. 15). Tiny, greenish yellow flowers appear in clusters in mid-summer. Origin, the Mediterranean area; it may have been introduced by the Romans.

Uses Strong yeast/celery aroma and flavour from entire plant the whole of which (except the roots) is used in cooking, especially for soups and casseroles, giving a yeast like flavour. Medicinal uses included relief of eye troubles, as a gargle and mouthwash, and as a deodorant, using the leaves in bath water.

History The common name is a corruption from *levisticum* by way of love-ache, its only name some centuries ago. The generic name itself is a corruption of *Ligisticum*, from Liguria, in Italy. It is reputed to have been of help in romantic troubles, and was grown regularly in herb gardens until the last century.

Cultivation Sow the seeds when ripe in late summer to early autumn as the period of viability is short, and transplant the following spring to 1 m (3 ft) apart, in moist well drained soil. Mulch every year. Also increase from root cuttings, each with an eye, in spring, put 5 cm (2 in) below soil level.

Fig. 16 Golden Marjoram

Fig. 17 Mint

Marjoram, sweet or knotted (*Origanum majorana; Labiatae*)
Description A half-hardy annual 20 cm (8 in) tall, rather bushy with small greyish green slightly hairy leaves, and round green 'knots' from which tiny pinkish flowers come from early summer onwards (Fig. 16). Origin, North Africa, introduced 1573. *O. vulgare* is a native plant of chalk downland.

Uses Sweet and unusual aroma to the leaves, which are much used, both fresh and dried, in cooking; especially good for flavouring sausages. Also used in perfumery and has mild antiseptic qualities, due to the thymol content.

History It was used a greal deal by the Greeks and may well have been introduced by the Romans though the official date is much later. Culpeper said that 'it is so well known that it is needless to give any description of it', so it must have been in every garden in the 17th century. Now much used in Italy.

Cultivation Sow seed outdoors in rows 30 cm (12 in) apart, in mid spring, earlier in warm sheltered gardens, and thin to 25 cm (10 in) apart. Provide a sunny place, and fertile, medium soil. Seedlings are slow to grow; weeding is important. Good for pot cultivation, but pot marjoram (*O. onites*) will be needed for winter use. This is perennial, but less well flavoured. Trim hard back in late summer and pot up in autumn.

Mint (*Mentha* species; *Labiatae*)
Description Perennial, mostly hardy herbaceous plants, with wide-spreading roots, stems to 30–60 cm (1–2 ft), and rounded or pointed leaves (Fig. 17). Inconspicuous purplish or white flowers in mid-late summer. Species cultivated: *M. spicata,* common mint, spearmint; *M. rotundifolia*, apple mint, smelling of apples; *M. × citrata* 'Eau de Cologne'; *M. rotundifolia* 'Variegata', green and cream edged leaves; pineapple mint, will not survive winter cold and damp. *M. × piperita*, pepper mint; *M. aquatica*, water mint. Origin, Europe including Britain.

Uses Mainly culinary, the leaves having varying fragrances and flavours as above. Leaves contain menthol and are good for summer drinks, and *M. citrata* is said to be an ingredient of Chartreuse liqueur. *M. piperita* leaves make a good digestive tea, so also does *M. aquatica*. Pepper mint is a popular flavouring much used in confectionery.

The bright blue, nodding flowers of borage (*Borago officinalis*) are extremely attractive to honey bees. Both the flowers and the rough, hairy leaves taste of cucumber.

This small, formal garden benefits from the shelter of tall beech hedges. Fragrant lilies add height to the low-growing herbs.

History Used by the Greeks and Romans, mentioned in the Bible, and widely used in Britain since at least the 9th century, when it was included in the monastic list of herbs. It has always been popular in this country up to, and including, the present day. Chaucer mentioned it in a poem, and Culpeper said that 'Applied with salt, it helps the bites of mad dogs'.

Cultivation Plant between autumn and spring; propagate by division at these seasons also, or lift rooted stems and plant these. Damp soil is preferred, but it grows so easily that it needs curbing rather than encouraging, except for pineapple mint, which is slow to grow and less vigorous. It is advisable to root cuttings of this and keep them in the greenhouse through the winter; all will grow well in containers. If rust infects the plants (small red-brown spots on leaves and stems), destroy them and plant afresh in a different place.

Oregano (Wild marjoram, *Origanum vulgare; Labiatae*)
Description Oregano is the Italian form of the native British wild marjoram. Both have the same botanic name, but the Italian plant has smoky-flavoured leaves, very hot-tasting if eaten raw. A perennial with tough creeping rootstock to 30 cm (12 in) long; slightly hairy, dark green, ovate leaves 1.5–5 cm (½–2 in) long in pairs on stems 30–75 cm (12–30 in) tall, and tiny pink-purple flowers in clusters from late summer to mid-autumn. Origin: Europe, Iran and Himalaya.

Uses Innumerable uses, especially in Provencal and Italian dishes; meat casseroles, soups, pizzas, quiches, tomato dishes of all kinds, egg dishes, mushrooms, sausages, and baked or grilled fish. Also has digestive action and antiseptic use.

History Oregano was used in cooking by the Greeks and Romans. It was much used medicinally by the monks in Britain in the 13th century to relieve toothache and headache, and also as hot fomentations for swellings and rheumatic pains. For two centuries, from Tudor times, it was a strewing herb for floors, then became even more popular medicinally.

Cultivation Provide a warm sunny place and well-drained chalky or stony soil. Grow from seed sown outdoors in mid-spring, or from cuttings taken in early summer, or by division in spring or early autumn. Space plants 50 cm (20 in) apart. Protect in winter with light covering of straw or bracken.

Parsley (*Petroselinum crispum; Umbelliferae*)
Description A hardy biennial usually grown as an annual, to about 45 cm (1½ ft) by 15 cm (6 in) wide; it is thinly taprooted with very much cut and curled leaves, and tiny green-yellow flowers in flat-headed clusters from early to late summer (Fig. 18). Origin, central and southern Europe; naturalised in Britain.

Uses Leaves strong and distinctive flavour, widely used in cooking. It contains an appreciable quantity of vitamin C, so has useful nutritional quality, and stimulates the digestion. Parsley water is said to be good for encouraging the disappearance of freckles.

History Parsley was used daily in ancient Greece, and it seems likely that the Romans introduced it to Britain, though officially it arrived in 1548, being brought here from Sardinia. Its reputation for slow

Fig. 18 Parsley

germination is said to be because it goes to the Devil seven times and back before sprouting. The common name is a corruption of petroselinum, via *petersylinge* and *perseli*.

Cultivation Sow in early to mid-spring for a summer crop in moist fertile soil and sun or shade; rows should be 30 cm (1 ft) apart, with 15 cm (6 in) in the row. A warm soil will speed germination, which can take 10–28 days. For winter use, sow in mid-summer, and protect in winter with cloches if snow is likely. Remove flowerheads to encourage leaves. It is a good container herb; for pots a 12 cm (5 in) size is best.

Rosemary *(Rosmarinus officinalis; Labiatae)*
Description An evergreen shrub hardy except in severe weather and

Fig. 19 Rosemary

wet soils, to about 120 cm (4 ft) in gardens by about 150 cm (5 ft) (Fig. 19). Very narrow, dark green leaves 2½ cm (1 in) long, and pale flowers in late spring. Origin, southern Europe and Asia Minor, probably introduced in the Middle Ages.

Uses The leaves are pungently and pleasantly aromatic giving a distinctive flavour in cooking; the oil contained in them is similar to eucalyptus. Rosemary is said to have an invigorating effect, and helps in restoring energy. It can also be used to improve the condition of skin and hair.

History The name comes from the Latin *ros* dew, and *maris* the sea – it grows naturally near the sea. Greek students twined it in their hair to help them think at examinations, and it was used in Greece at weddings, christenings and funerals. It was thought to be a disinfectant, even against the Plague.

Cultivation Plant in a sunny place and well-drained soil in spring; regular use will do all the pruning necessary. Easily increased from tip cuttings taken in early spring, putting four in a 10 cm (4 in) pot in a frame or greenhouse. Later cuttings in late summer are also possible.

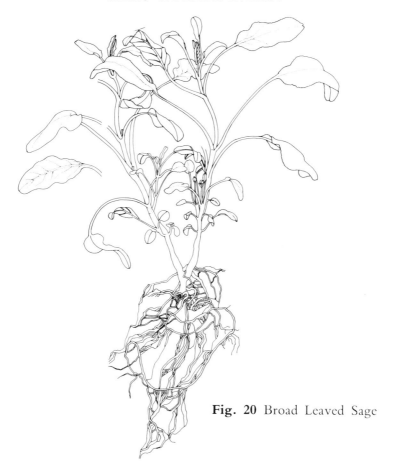

Fig. 20 Broad Leaved Sage

Sage *(Salvia officinalis; Labiatae)*

Description An evergreen shrub, hardy except in severe winters and damp soil. Height: 60 cm (2 ft) with the same spread. Grey-green, wrinkled, slightly woolly leaves, with blue-purple or white flowers in early summer (Fig. 20). Origin, southern Europe and the Mediterranean area, introduced in 1597 or earlier.

Uses The strongly aromatic, slightly bitter leaves are much used in cooking, in particular with pork or duck. Sage tea is said to be good for gargling and as a mouth wash; it helps in the digestion, and in clearing a stuffy head if the steam from an infusion is inhaled.

History The name comes from the Latin *salveo*, to save or to heal, and it was considered by the Romans to be a veritable cure-all, and very much the most effective of all the medicinal herbs. An Arabic proverb says 'How can a man die who has sage in his garden?' The Greeks regarded it as a sacred herb, and it was even thought, during the 17th century, to delay the onset of symptoms of old age.

Cultivation Plant in spring in well-drained, moderately fertile soil and a sunny place. A heavy wet soil is to be avoided. Easily grown from seed sown in mid-spring, which takes about three weeks to germinate; also increased from 8 cm (3 in) cuttings taken in late summer and put in a cold frame. Pot on singly and plant out the following spring.

Salad burnet (*Poterium sanguisorba; Rosaceae*)
Description A decorative, hardy, herbaceous perennial, low growing, with flower stems to 30–45 cm (1–1½ ft). The toothed leaves are pinnate and nearly evergreen, and red-tinted round heads of tiny green flowers come all summer. Origin, Europe, native to this country.

Uses Mainly for the leaves which are cucumber flavoured, and put in salads, soups and drinks. Used in the same way as borage. Also said to have value as a tonic.

History The name is derived from the latin *sanguis*, blood and *sobere*, to soak up; there is a story that a Hungarian king gave orders for the juice of the plant to be used on the wounds of 15,000 of his soldiers after a battle. The Greeks grew it, also for medical purposes. First deliberately cultivated in the 16th century in this country. Culpeper, in the 17th century, thought it had 'a drying and an astringent quality . . . to staunch bleedings inward or outward'.

Cultivation Easily grown, salad burnet prefers light soil. Sow seed when ripe in summer, or the following spring, thinning plants to 23 cm (9 in) apart. Established plants can be increased by division in early spring. It makes a good container herb.

Savory (*Satureja* species: *Labiatae*)
Description *Satureja hortensis,* summer savory; an annual plant to 20 cm (8 in) with narrow leaves 1 cm (½ in) long, and pale lilac flowers in spikes from mid-summer to early autumn S. *montana*, winter savory; a hardy perennial, semi-evergreen, sub-shrub to 35 cm (15 in), otherwise similar to summer savory. Origin, southern Europe, introduced around 1562, or earlier.

Uses Leaves are strongly aromatic, nearer to a spice than a herb, used in cooking, mainly to flavour beans, but also in salads, soups and with fish; gather the leaves before the flowers appear. The savories are good bee plants. The leaves are sometimes used to help in digestion. Is said to ward off blackfly from broad beans if grown with them.

History Vinegar flavoured with savory was as much used by the Romans as mint sauce is used by us. The word *satureja* is thought to come from satyr, the plant being once considered as an aphrodisiac. The leaves were said to alleviate the pain of bee and wasp stings.

Cultivation Summer savory is grown from seed sown in mid-spring in rows 30 cm (1 ft) apart, thinned to 15 cm (6 in). The leaves can be gathered twice, in late summer and in mid-autumn, for drying. Cover the seed lightly, otherwise germination is poor. Winter savory can also be grown from seed, by division in spring, or from 5 cm (2 in) cuttings taken in late spring, put in a frame, and then potted on and planted out the following spring.

Sorrel, French or buckler-leaved (*Rumex scutatus; Polygonaceae*)

Description A hardy perennial, rather sprawling plant, dying down every autumn; height of flowering stems to 30 cm (1 ft), with similar spread. Leaves are rounded shield shaped, about 4 cm (1½ in) wide, slightly fleshy; insignificant greenish flowers appear in sumer. Origin, Europe, North Africa, West Asia; introduced but sometimes naturalised in this country (Fig. 21).

Uses The rather sour leaves are very good for soup, but otherwise should be used sparingly for flavouring as they are very strong tasting. Also said to have diuretic qualities and to contain vitamin C.

History Culpeper said that the leaves of all the sorrels were of 'great use against scurvy if eaten in spring as salads'; the Greeks and Romans were convinced of their use in kidney troubles. Sorrels were popular medical herbs but parts of the plants contain oxalic acid, and the leaves should therefore be used sparingly.

Cultivation Plant in spring or early autumn in moist, slightly heavy soil allowing 30 cm (1 ft) between the plants; remove the flowering stems to encourage leaf production. Divide in spring or sow seeds in mid-spring, thinning when large enough to handle.

Fig. 21 Sorrel

Sweet Cicely (*Myrrhis odorata; Umbelliferae*)
Description A hardy perennial to 90–150 cm (3–5 ft) when 8–10 years old, with many thick tenacious roots like an octopus. Delicate fern-like, large leaves and tiny white flowers in umbel-like clusters late spring to early summer; dark brown-black, narrow seeds 2 cm (¾ in) long mid to late summer. Native to Britain and Europe.

Uses Whole plant strong aniseed flavour, leaves sweet-tasting as well. Use them to replace up to half the sugar in tart fruit dishes – more will give overwhelming flavour of aniseed – and mix with fruit or vegetable salads, or with butter to produce herb butter; boil roots with oil and lemon and serve as side vegetable; useful as a sugar substitute for diabetics or slimmers. Has slight antiseptic property.

History Once known as seseli which was commuted to the modern spelling as sweet Ciceley, and was once also called sweet bracken or sweet fern. The Latin words *myrrhis* and *odorata* mean respectively perfume and fragrant. Its use in Britain dates back at least to Roman times – it was once called the Roman plant – and it had some use in healing ointments.

Cultivation Sow seeds late winter-late spring or late summer-mid autumn. Must have cold period of 0–5° C (32–40° F) to ensure germination, so put seeds to be sown in spring in the refrigerator, mixed with sand, for 6–8 weeks. Provide partial shade, and deep moist acid-neutral soil. Space 60 cm (2 ft) apart. Increase by self-sown seedlings or by root cuttings, each with an 'eye' (bud), placed 5 cm (2 in) below the surface, in autumn or winter. Use thicker parts of roots.

Tansy (*Chrysanthemum* or *Tanacetum vulgare; Compositae*)

Description A hardy herbaceous perennial to 60 cm (2 ft), with toothed leaves cut almost pinnately, up to 12 cm (5 in) long, and small, flat heads of yellow flowers from mid-summer (Fig. 22). Origin, Europe, native to this country. There is a curled leaved form.

Uses The leaves are strongly aromatic, rather like camphor, and can be used in the same way that mint is with roast lamb; they have many other culinary uses. Tansy tea was used for colds and rheumatism, and a distillation of the leaves is said to be good for the complexion, removing freckles and sunburn.

History The common name comes from athanasia, or immortality, so it must originally have been thought to have much medicinal virtue. Tansy puddings were very popular in Elizabethan days, but might be considered very bitter now. However, an old recipe for this includes brandy and syrup of roses, so it is possible that it might be palatable!

Cultivation Easily grown, as would be expected of a native plant; any soil and situation will suit it. Division of the plant in spring is the usual method of increase, putting pieces 30 cm (1 ft) apart. It needs controlling, otherwise spread is rapid.

Tarragon (*Artemisia dracunculus; Compositae*)

Description A semi-evergreen perennial, hardy unless the weather is

Fig. 22 Tansy

very cold or the soil badly drained, particularly in winter; to 60 cm (2 ft) tall, spreading to 60 cm (2 ft) also. Leaves narrow and linear, with insignificant greyish flowers. The French variety is the best to grow because of its flavour. Origin, southern Europe, introduced 1548.

Uses The leaves have an unusual and particularly pleasing flavour, reminiscent of cloves, but with delicate overtones, and are used to make tarragon vinegar and for all sorts of savoury dishes. Also for sauce tartare and Continental mustard.

History Although a very popular herb in culinary quarters, it has virtually no medical history; the common name is derived from the French *estragon*, a little dragon – it was thought to be of use in healing the stings of venomous animals. In Tudor days, it was grown only in the Royal gardens.

Cultivation A well-drained, even dryish soil is essential, and preferably a sunny sheltered place, though an exposed site will do, if the soil is light. Plant in spring or early autumn at 60 cm (2 ft) apart, and transplant about four years after the original planting, to maintain the flavour. Increase by division in spring. Seed does not set in this country. Protect in severe weather. Container cultivation is not easy, but the skilled gardener may like to pot up a few plants.

Thyme (*Thymus vulgaris; Labiatae*)
Description Common thyme is a hardy evergreen shrublet to 20 cm (8 in) tall, spreading to 30 cm (1 ft) and more (Fig. 23); tiny leaves, and lilac coloured flowers from early to late summer. *T × citriodorus* is similar but with broader, lemon-scented leaves. Origin, southern Europe, introduced before 1548.

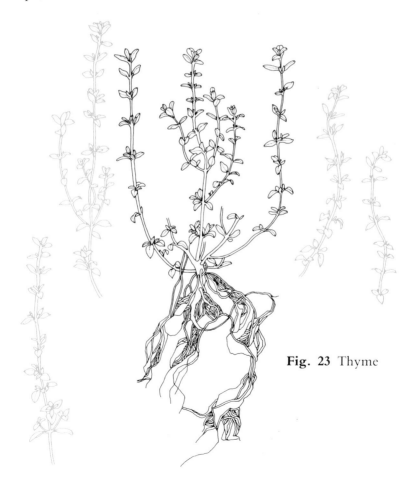

Fig. 23 Thyme

Herbs can be mixed with border plants. Ornamental grey-leaved *stachys lanata* blends well with cream and green variegated apple mint in the foreground.

Uses Considerable culinary use for the highly aromatic leaves, particularly with meat and savoury dishes generally, and in Benedictine liqueur, also lemon thyme in custard. The essential oil, thymol, is the part which helps coughs and catarrh. Thyme is said to have considerable germicidal action. Also good for baths, and is used in toothpaste. Lemon thyme is used in perfumery.

History Extensively grown by the Greeks and Romans, it was probably brought to this country by the latter, who prescribed it as a cure for melancholy. The Greeks regarded it as an emblem for courage and an infusion was even recommended in 1633 for a cure for shyness. It has a considerable medical use today, so altogether it is essential to any herb garden.

Cultivation Easily grown by dividing in spring, or from 5 cm (2 in) long cuttings taken in early summer, put in a frame, potted on when rooted, and planted out in early autumn. Seed is sown in spring (not lemon thyme) and treated in the same way, the final distance between plants being 30 cm (1 ft) either way. A sunny place and a light soil are preferred, preferably alkaline. It is a good container plant.

CHAPTER 4

HARVESTING, PRESERVING AND STORING HERBS

With a supply of herbs in your garden and the knowledge of how to harvest, preserve and store them, you can make sure of having the flavours you require for cooking throughout the year. What's more, you will be able to turn to your winter store for beauty aids and soothing drinks when fresh herbs are unobtainable. Preserving herbs is not difficult. There was a time when every housewife would know about such things. Drying is the most commonly used method and is very good, and those who own a home-freezer will find that many basic herbs can be 'put on ice' so to speak until they are needed.

Harvesting might sound a rather grandiose word if you have but a few herbs in pots on your window ledge, but it applies just as much to gathering in a few stems as it does to vast quantities. In any case, you must never pick or cut more herbs to be dried – or frozen – at any one time than can easily be dealt with.

Where the leaves are to be preserved cut just before the herb comes into flower. The reason for this is that much of the strength of the plant would go into the flowers and you wouldn't get such a tasty end-product. Left until after the flowers have faded you get the problem of what to do with the stems and seeds. If the worst comes to the worst and you return from a holiday to find the season more advanced than you expected and the herbs already in flower, you can still manage, even mixing flowers and leaves in together. This will not give a first-class result, either for colour or flavour, but would 'do'.

Herbs should not be cut on a wet day; choose a bright sunny one. Leave it until after the dew has disappeared so the foliage is dry, and pick before the sun gets very hot.

Using a sharp implement, where necessary, you can cut the stems of small-leaved plants to make life easier for drying and dealing with the herb later on. Large leaves can be picked individually but whatever you do, be careful not to damage them, especially such fragrant ones as lemon balm which suffer from bruising.

Marjoram and thyme are easy herbs to dry. When picking basil always keep some leaves on the plant as this seems to encourage others to grow. Be careful leaves do not darken. If drying in bunches, 2–3 sprigs per bunch, no more. Borage is not a simple herb to dry, nor is chervil. Chives are far better used fresh or frozen. Dill and fennel leaves can be dried but are best for their seeds. Parsley requires care, and should be picked before it bolts.

Plants from which the seeds are to be harvested should be left until the heads turn brown. You have to watch your timing carefully or the seeds will fall and scatter. Better be early than late. Pick on a dry day. Caraway, coriander, dill, fennel and lovage are good for their seeds.

Chamomile flowers are dried for making into teas, pot-pourri and so on. Other herbal flowers, such as tansy, can also be dried. Pick them on a dry day before they are fully opened.

Garlic is something of an exception as far as drying herbs is concerned. Harvest in the autumn. Leave it on top of the ground or in a warm, (not hot) dry atmosphere until ready, then store in a cool, airy place as you do onions.

Angelica stems for candying must be young and tender; get ready for that in mid to late spring.

Herbs that are to be home-frozen should be picked when young and very fresh, and dealt with as quickly as possible. They should be clean. If necessary wash thoroughly.

Drying really means that the herbs need to be in a steady warm temperature with the dry air circulating all the time to take away moisture, and there should be no risk of condensation. Drying in the sun, which might sound tempting, is not always effective and can mar the colour. Generally, the more quickly herbs are dried the more of their aroma is preserved.

Most homes have plenty of suitable spots. An attic which is warmed by the sun, that is clean and airy and which doesn't suffer from quick heat loss at night; a spare room; an airing cupboard; the cooker; the kitchen: a garage which is not likely to be filled with petrol fumes, can all be used successfully; always avoid placing herbs in the sun's rays.

You can tie herbs, keeping each variety to itself, in bunches and hang them up to dry. Keep bundles small. They could become mildewed in the middle if too full. When there is a danger of their becoming dusty, cover them with fine muslin.

Bunches take between 14–21 days to get crisp and brittle, at which stage they are ready to be prepared for storing.

An alternative method is to have drying trays ready. These can be wooden frames with a fine mesh base, or home-made from cake trays or roasting tins, over which butter muslin is stretched. Lay the leaves or sprigs a little way from each other. You can layer trays in an airing cupboard, as long as you know there won't be any damp clothes put in, too, and by leaving a gap between the layers the air can move freely.

Laying herbs in bunches or hanging them in a very cool oven can be both successful and speedy. The temperature should be as low as possible; if necessary keep the door ajar. If you can't get the temperature low leave the trays outside the oven with the door open, or hang herbs above the cooker. As soon as the herbs are ready, let them cool before storing.

Parsley is not an easy herb to dry, you have to be watchful with it, but is easy to freeze.

There are various schools of thought about the best way of coping with parsley, and it is by trial and error you arrive at the method that you like best. The secret is to keep colour and flavour successfully. There are those who maintain it must be plunged into boiling water in which a pinch of bicarbonate of soda has been added before it is dried. Others prefer it absolutely dry, and yet others who insist on plunging it into boiling water for a few seconds to make sure no insects are lurking inside the foliage.

You can hang one or two bunches of parsley in a hot oven, 200° C (400° F), Mark 6, for up to one minute, then reduce heat to lowest possible setting (below a quarter on gas cooker) and leave the oven door ajar until the parsley is brittle. If you do this make sure the parsley does not scorch.

Or you can hang it, or lay it on trays, in the oven at 110° C (225° F), Mark ¼, for about an hour and then leave it in a very cool oven until it is crisp.

Another way is to leave it on trays outside the oven with the temperature at 130°–140° C (250°–275° F), Mark ½–1, until it is ready.

Herbs can also be dried, very quickly, in a microwave oven, but care has to be taken not to over-cook them. Well wash and gently pat dry with kitchen paper. Only dry one kind of herb at a time. Remove thick stalks where necessary (bay leaves should be taken from the stem). Place herb on kitchen paper, cover with another piece of kitchen paper and put into the microwave together with a small bowl of water. On full power reckon on 4–7 minutes per ounce of herbs. Some take longer than others so check constantly. Also ensure the water does not completely evaporate.

All of these methods work.

Seeds have to be looked after, too. Cut the tops off the plants with the seed heads attached and lay them carefully on prepared trays, then cover with clean, dry pieces of linen or cotton and leave in a warm, airy room until the seeds loosen. Beat out the seeds with a stick and lay them to dry in a warm spot where the temperature must not go above

21° C (70° F). Turn them over daily. When fully dry they can be stored.

If you want to retain the natural cream colour of chamomile flowers – which is delightful – pick them when they are dry and lay them in a warm place on trays, and turn them daily to prevent them lumping together.

Candying is another way of preserving, and for this flowers are usually chosen, but perhaps angelica is one of the best known of all, and for this you use the young, tender stems. To crystallise your angelica takes about two weeks, but if you do some for gifts as well, you will be making charming as well as more unusual presents for your friends.

Choose stems that are bright in colour and cut into 8 cm (3 in) long pieces. Immerse in a boiling brine solution 10 g (¼ oz) salt to 2.5 ltr (4 pts) water; leave to soak for 10 minutes, drain and rinse in cold water. Pop back into fresh boiling water, simmer until tender, 5–10 minutes. Remove, drain and scrape away outer skin.

Weigh the stems. For every pound allow 175 g (6 oz) sugar and 300 ml (½ pint) water. Dissolve sugar in the water, bring to boiling point, pour over stems. If there isn't sufficient syrup make more in the same way. Leave 24 hours. Drain syrup off, add 50 g (2 oz) more sugar to it, bring to boil, pour over stems, leave 24 hours. Repeat this process daily until the 8th day. On the 8th day add 75 g (3 oz) sugar and the stems to the syrup, boil for 3–4 minutes, return to bowl and leave 48 hours. On the 10th day repeat this process, by which time the syrup should be the consistency of honey when cold. Leave 4 days, Dry off in a cool oven, 36° C (100°–120° F), or less than Mark ¼ with the door ajar.

When it is cold, store the angelica between layers of waxed paper in a clean, air-tight container.

Before you get around to storing herbs you must make sure you have an adequate supply of containers. Small glass jars with tight-fitting lids or corks are ideal, and these must be spotlessly clean and dry.

If you intend to keep herbs on the sprig (sage, thyme, rosemary are excellent for this and useful for making bunches of herbs, or for putting into vinegars or oils as decoration) you do need suitable-sized jars.

You do for bay too, if you want to keep that on the stalk and pick leaves off as required. Bay leaves have a tendency to curl up at the edges. Should you be fussy, you can lay them, once they are dry, under a board for about 10 days to flatten. Bay leaves can be stored crumbled, whole or crushed. Whole is probably more useful as you can always break off as much as you want at any one time.

Removing leaves from herb sprigs once they are brittle is very easy. So large or small leaves can be crumbled or crushed, whichever way you prefer. Crumbled preserves the flavour longer, crushed and then powdered is easier for quick seasonings. To powder, roll crumbled leaves with a rolling pin and then rub through a fine hair sieve. Jar immediately.

There is a measure of insurance attached to using glass jars. It is easy to see if moisture appears in them. Should this happen, the contents could not have been dried sufficiently, so tip them out on to greaseproof paper or muslin and dry again.

Store the jars in a dark, cool place, or wrap dark blue paper round them, or use opaque jars. Label them clearly with the name of the herb and the date on which it was packed.

Dried herbs and seeds should be effective for up to one year. Some last better than others, though. Rosemary, sage, marjoram and basil, for instance, can be used for longer, whereas tarragon and lemon balm can begin to lose something of their flavour after about nine months.

Seeds are best stored whole and crushed (or powdered) immediately before use.

There are various ways you can home-freeze herbs; to a certain extent it depends on how you want to use them. Whichever your method, wash, dry and freeze as quickly as possible.

One way is to snip chives with scissors, or chop mint, or borage or parsley, or whatever herb you want, lay it in ice cube trays, cover with cold water and freeze. Remove the cubes, wrap each one separately and bag or box together in herbs of one kind. Label clearly and date.

These cubes served in drinks (see recipes) are often time-saving, apart from being decorative. You can add ice cubes straight into your sauces and casseroles.

Another way is to lay sprigs or leaves out on foil in the fast-freeze section and bag or box when frozen, making sure that all the air is expelled. Or, you can place the washed, dried herbs straight into containers, again making sure the air is all out, and freeze. Parsley frozen on the sprig crumbles immediately when rubbed in your fingers.

Frozen herbs will keep successfully for up to six months.

Thawed sprigs are not recommended for garnish. They look rather limp and sorry for themselves.

CHAPTER 5

COOKING WITH HERBS

Growing your own herbs provides you with a splendid opportunity to be adventurous in your cooking. You can blend different flavours in stews and casseroles, create exciting sauces for fish, meat and pasta dishes, add interest to salads, to egg and cheese recipes, and make puddings and cakes, biscuits and breads that will be the envy of all your friends.

With herbs you can garnish and decorate to provide eye-appeal to your culinary creations and it is important that a dish looks as good as it tastes.

Certain herbs have become associated with different foods. Be guided, but not dominated, by this association. You have to experiment for yourself. Start with small quantities, as over–flavouring is unsatisfactory. A herb should complement and blend into a recipe, not be an overpowering element in it; and the amount that suits one person might not please another. So using 'a pinch', that is a quarter of a level teaspoonful, makes sense as a beginning.

You will also have to adjust the quantities according to whether you are using freshly picked, dried or frozen herbs, and realise that some are far more strongly flavoured than others.

Generally speaking, dried have a more concentrated flavour than fresh herbs, so use less; frozen ones don't have quite such a pronounced taste as those taken straight from the garden, so you might have to use more.

Parsley, mint, lemon thyme can be used without too much thought; chives too, if you like a slightly oniony touch.

Chervil, tarragon, thyme, bay leaves, savory, lovage, marjoram, oregano and hyssop have strong flavours and should be used sparingly.

Among well-known cookery terms that can bemuse inexperienced cooks are 'a bunch of herbs', 'a bouquet garni', 'aux fines herbes' and 'mixed herbs'. These terms can also stifle your imagination and ingenuity if you believe they are unalterable.

A bunch of herbs is not really any different from a bouquet garni. You make a bunch of herbs when you tie small sprigs of herbs with cotton or string to the handle of the pan and allow them to cook with other ingredients. They can easily be removed before dishing up. The sprigs recommended are parsley and thyme and a bay leaf. A bouquet garni can be exactly the same, or it can be thyme, parsley and bay leaf put in a muslin bag with three or four peppercorns.

The important thing is that you can make your own mixtures; rosemary, savory, marjoram, chervil, basil are all very suitable. Make the most of whatever you have available.

When a recipe calls for 'aux fines herbes', and this is usually for an egg or salad dish or a sauce, it generally means equal quantities of finely chopped chervil, parsley, tarragon and chives. But 'fines herbes' can also be a combination of three or more perfumed herbs, so you can take your pick.

'Mixed herbs' generally refers to thyme, marjoram, parsley and savory.

Make the most of herbs for salads. The fresh foliage, finely chopped, can make an amazing difference and flowers of bergamot or borage add colour as well. You can also make excellent dressings that are your own, exclusive 'blend'. For instance, add a handful of chopped mixed herbs, such as chives, tarragon, chervil or salad burnet, to a standard salad cream, mayonnaise, natural yogurt or vinegar about 30 minutes before it is to be used. Add finely chopped, mixed herbs to soured cream, seasoning to taste, and adding a little lemon juice, on another occasion.

You can make your own seasonings for stews and soups and so on, by blending dried, powdered herbs.

A Victorian aromatic seasoning is: 75 g (3 oz) each basil, marjoram and thyme, 50 g (2 oz) each winter savory and peppercorns, 25 g (1 oz) each bay leaves, mace, nutmeg, cloves, 15 g (½ oz) dried, grated lemon peel. Pound them all together, sieve finely and store. Adding 5 ml (1 teaspoon) powdered garlic makes a stronger flavour still. Use in quantities as required.

A useful seasoning for egg and chicken recipes is: 15 ml (1 tablespoon) each dried powdered summer savory, tarragon, chervil and basil.

Aromatic mixtures such as these are easy to make, so never attempt to store one for too long; the flavour can deteriorate. The use of sauces in cooking is invaluable. Here in Britain, we tend to be somewhat stereotyped with our use of herbs for them. Parsley sauce is perhaps the best known and very good it is too, especially with fish or broad beans. You get the best flavour from it if the parsley is chopped (it must be dry, otherwise the sauce will become coloured) and added after the sauce is made. You can toss in as much as you like.

But chervil can be used as a change; indeed, chervil makes an easy substitute for parsley in any case.

Finely chopped fresh fennel leaves are another alternative to parsley. This sauce is delicious with fish.

When housewives were unable to rush down to the nearest supermarket they had to rely on flavourings that were easily available. As a result they used their garden 'store cupboard'.

Here are some examples that are well worth trying. Put one or two bay leaves with milk to warm, not boil, and then allow to cool. Make rice, sago puddings with this milk. It is very good for custards, as well. Treat lemon verbena in a similar fashion for a baked custard.

Keep a bay leaf in a jar or tin with caster sugar. The sugar will add flavour to puddings and cakes.

To an apple pie recipe that includes cinnamon, add half a teaspoon crushed coriander seeds. Another tasty pie idea is to sprinkle a few seeds in with apple slices for a pie or tart.

Rhubarb is quite sharp, even when sweetened, but if you cook it with a few pieces of young, tender angelica stems (not candied angelica) much of the tartness will disappear.

Try just a pinch of powdered coriander in a summer junket.

For cakes and breads and biscuits, add your own herb flavourings; for instance, sprinkle coriander or caraway seeds on top of a loaf or cake; add one teaspoon powdered rosemary to a standard biscuit mixture. Mix caraway seeds into a dough.

With so much said nowadays about cutting down our sugar intake, it is good to know there is a herb that will help us do just that. Sweet Cicely is not called 'sweet' for nothing. By adding freshly chopped leaves to tart fruit pies, fresh fruit salads or to fruit puddings you can reduce the quantity of sugar used.

Indeed, making the most of herbs is almost an endless task. For example, add a little chopped chervil to batter when you are frying fish, or a pinch of dried thyme into the pancake mixture when it is for a savoury meal. Add a little sage to the batter for a sausage toad-in-the-hole.

Plainly cooked white fish can be on the boring side, not though if you add fennel, lemon thyme and marjoram to the milk in which the fish is boiled. While on the subject of fish, tinned salmon or tuna, mixed with mayonnaise, sprinkled with dill seeds, served on cracker biscuits are easy canapés.

Lovage, which is quite powerfully flavoured, makes an ideal alternative for celery in soups and stews.

Bay is strongly flavoured, and to begin with only uses ½ leaf per two people. Use it when boiling bacon for extra good flavour.

All fresh herbs can be used for garnish, and, remember, making a dish look attractive helps to make it more appetising. Chopped dried herbs can also be sprinkled over dishes to give them extra flavour and greater eye-appeal.

Parsley is frequently used as a garnish. Perhaps this was because there was a time when parsley was regarded as an antidote to poison, so putting a sprig or two on each serving plate was a sign that no harm was intended to one's guests!

Now let us have a look at which herbs to use with what.

Beef:	Horseradish, basil, marjoram, thyme, rosemary.
Pork and Bacon:	Sage, basil, rosemary, chives, parsley, bay, dill.
Lamb:	Rosemary, garlic, summer savory, dill, bay, oregano, coriander leaf.
Veal:	Thyme, sage, rosemary, lemon verbena, lemon balm, oregano.
Stews:	Bay, dill, garlic, horseradish, marjoram, parsley, thyme, oregano, hyssop (use sparingly), lovage (sparingly), sage, rosemary, tarragon, chives, coriander seeds (and for curries).
Soups:	Basil (especially for tomato or turtle), mint (especially for pea), parsley, thyme, bay, fennel (for fish). Nettles and sorrel make soups in their own right.
Poultry:	Parsley, sage, summer savory, tarragon, thyme, rosemary, fennel.
Fish:	Fennel, sage, parsley, basil, chives, chervil.
Eggs:	Chives, tarragon, chervil, marjoram, basil, parsley, salad burnet (especially for omelets).
Hard Cheeses:	Basil, thyme, chervil, sage.
Soft Cheeses:	Mint, dill, sage, basil, caraway, chives, garlic, parsley.
Goats' and Ewes' cheeses:	Oregano and herbs as above.
Salads:	Salad burnet, chives, borage, fennel, basil, tarragon, chervil, thyme, lemon balm, garlic, sage, angelica leaves, dill foliage.
Pasta:	Basil, chervil, garlic, mint, parsley, thyme, oregano.

Pizzas:	Oregano, basil, marjoram, thyme, garlic.
Cabbage:	Parsley, fennel, caraway, finely chopped borage – added just before serving.
Peas:	Summer savory, mint.
Carrots:	Summer savory, mint, basil, parsley.
Potatoes:	Mint, parsley, chives, garlic, dill.
Spinach:	Mint, summer savory.
Beans:	Summer savory, sage, parsley.
Tomatoes:	Basil, marjoram, chives, parsley, oregano, lemon balm.
Stuffings:	Parsley, sage, thyme (lemon thyme good with veal), chervil.
Sauces:	Bay, dill (for fish), fennel (for fish), garlic, mint, parsley, horseradish, chervil, angelica leaves (sweet sauce).
Teas and Vinegars:	As you wish, (tarragon famous for vinegar).
Breads, Cakes, Biscuits:	Caraway, coriander, rosemary, fennel (seeds), basil.
Desserts:	Mint, lemon verbena, bay, caraway, angelica, dill, tansy, sweet Cicely.
Jams and Jellies:	Lemon Verbena, mint, parsley.
Cold Drinks and Cups:	Borage and flowers, mint, lemon balm, rosemary, salad burnet, lovage, bergamot and flowers.
Garnishes:	Parsley, mint, thyme, rosemary, lemon balm, basil, chervil, savory, borage flowers, bergamot flowers, angelica, chives.

It would be wrong to finish this chapter without particular reference to sorrel and garlic.

The young leaves of sorrel can be cooked and eaten as a vegetable in the same way as spinach and can be used for soups.

Garlic, which can be used in all savoury dishes has a strong taste and powerful aroma. It is best to ask if guests like it, or use very carefully; too much can be off-putting. If you enjoy the pungency of garlic in a salad but have to be wary of others that do not share your taste, rub a cut clove of garlic round the inside of the salad bowl before adding the other ingredients. This will impart just a hint of flavour.

STARTERS

COUNTRY SOUP *8 helpings*

900 g (2 lb) potatoes, finely diced
25 g (1 oz) butter
30 ml (2 tablesp) oil
1 large leek, trimmed, chopped
1 medium-sized onion, chopped
2 carrots, chopped
100 g (4 oz) lentils
15 ml (1 tablesp) tomato purée

1.5 ltr (2½ pt) chicken or white
   vegetable stock
400 g (15 oz) can tomatoes
5 ml (1 teasp) oregano
15 ml (1 tablesp) chopped parsley
½ teasp celery salt
Salt and pepper to taste

GARNISH:
Bacon rashers, grilled until crisp,
   crumbled

Heat butter and oil in a large saucepan or pressure cooker. Add potatoes, leek, onion and carrots. Fry until vegetables start to colour. Stir in remaining ingredients. Break up tomatoes. Bring to boil and simmer for 1 hour. Alternatively, pressure cook, at high pressure, for 10 min. Spoon into warmed serving bowls. Garnish with bacon.

SCOTCH MARINADED MUSHROOMS *2–3 helpings*

30 ml (2 tablesp) whisky
45 ml (3 tablesp) oil
10 ml (2 teasp) lemon juice
½ level teasp fresh thyme

10 ml (2 teasp) chopped parsley
Pinch caster sugar
Salt and pepper
100 g (4 oz) button mushrooms,
   washed and dried

Mix together all ingredients, except mushrooms. Stir well. Put into a container with a lid. Add mushrooms and put on lid. Turn to coat the mushrooms with the liquid. Leave to stand for about 2 hours, turning the container from time to time to toss the mushrooms in the marinade. Serve the mushrooms with a little of the marinade. Accompany with fresh crusty bread.

Scotch marinaded mushrooms.

ASPARAGUS SAVOURY *4–6 helpings*

225 g (8 oz) fresh asparagus or
298 g (10½ oz) can asparagus
3 eggs, separated
142 ml (¼ pt) fresh double cream

175 g (6 oz) Cheddar cheese, grated
10 ml (2 teasp) chopped chives
5 ml (1 teasp) mustard powder
Salt and pepper

Pre-heat oven at 200° C, 400° F, Mark 6. Cook fresh asparagus and drain well. Lightly grease an ovenproof dish. Arrange most of the tinned or fresh asparagus in the base, reserving some for garnish. Whisk egg whites until stiff and fold in the egg yolks, cream, cheese, chives and mustard. Add salt and pepper to taste. Pour over the asparagus. Bake for about 25 min or until golden brown. Serve hot garnished with the reserved asparagus.

MINTED CUCUMBER JELLY *6–8 helpings*

2 cucumbers
284 ml (½ pt) water
1–2 sprigs fresh mint

10 ml (2 teasp) lemon juice
20 ml (4 teasp) powdered gelatine
Salt and pepper

Reserve a quarter of a cucumber. Peel and coarsely grate the rest of that cucumber and the other one. Simmer the pulp with the water, lemon juice and mint sprigs in a covered pan for 15 minutes. Remove mint. Sieve or blend cucumber mixture to make 568 ml (1 pt) thickish liquid. Season. Dissolve the gelatine in 75 ml (5 tablesp) of the mixture, add to rest, stir well. Thinly slice reserved, unpeeled, cucumber. Arrange ⅓ of the slices in the base of a wetted mould. Cover with ⅓ of the liquid jelly. Leave to set. Repeat with a further ⅓ of the slices and jelly. Leave to set. Finally, use up remaining ingredients. When firm, turn out on to a serving platter, surround with a salad garnish and serve with home-made mayonnaise.

TZATZIKI *4–6 helpings*

150 g (5 oz approx) pot thick set
   natural yogurt
½–1 glove garlic, crushed
Salt and freshly ground black pepper

15 ml (1 tablesp) finely chopped fresh
   mint
15 ml (1 tablesp) lemon juice
½ large cucumber, peeled, coarsely
   grated
¼ cucumber, unpeeled and coarsely
   grated

Mix garlic, seasoning, mint and lemon juice into yogurt. Cover and chill for at least 30 minutes. Meanwhile place grated cucumber (peeled and unpeeled) into a nylon sieve and leave to drain. Gently squeeze out any remaining liquid from the cucumber after it has stood for 20 min. Mix into yogurt. Serve either chilled or at room temperature, accompanied by hot pitta bread.

NB: In this sort of recipe quantities can be adapted to suit family tastes; i.e. more cucumber or mint, less yogurt or garlic.

CHEDDARED CHOICE *4 helpings*

100–175 g (4–6 oz) Cheddar cheese (preferably mature)	*Freshly ground black pepper*
50 g (2 oz) butter, softened	*5 ml (1 teasp) made mustard*
2 cloves garlic, chopped	*5 ml (1 teasp) dried herbs or*
Pinch salt	*10 ml (2 teasp) fresh herbs of choice*
	60 ml (4 tablesp) sherry

Crush the chopped garlic to a paste with the salt. Coarsely grate the cheese and work into the softened butter. Add the garlic, mustard and herbs, then beat in the sherry. Press into a small earthenware or china pot. Place a piece of waxed paper on the surface of the cheese, cover the dish with a tightly fitting lid or with foil and refrigerate for several hours before serving. Accompany with hot toast or oatcakes.

HORSERADISH AND BEEF SPREAD *4 helpings*

225 g (8 oz) lean, cold roast beef	*15 ml (1 tablesp) Worcestershire sauce*
50 g (2 oz) butter, softened	*15 ml (1 tablesp) brandy*
15 ml (1 tablesp) horseradish cream	*Salt and freshly ground black pepper to taste*
5 ml (1 teasp) grated horseradish	
1 clove garlic, crushed	GARNISH:
5 ml (1 teasp) made mustard	*Parsley sprigs*

Process beef and grated horseradish until smooth. Mix all ingredients thoroughly together. Transfer to a serving bowl. Serve at room temperature, garnished with parsley (or any herb of your choice). Accompany with fingers of hot, wholemeal toast.

SMOKED MACKEREL WITH
TARRAGON AND ORANGE SALAD *4 helpings*

450 g (1 lb) ready-to-eat smoked
  mackerel fillets

SALAD:
2 oranges, peeled
1 lemon, peeled

5 ml (1 teasp) Demerara sugar
10 ml (2 teasp) chopped tarragon
25 g (1 oz) chopped walnuts
1 bunch watercress
Oil and vinegar dressing

Prepare the salad. Remove any pith from oranges and lemon, then thinly slice the fruit. Discard any thick stalks from the watercress. Place fruit in a serving bowl. Sprinkle sugar and tarragon over. Mix in nuts and watercress. Shortly before serving toss in the oil and vinegar dressing. Arrange fish fillets on individual serving plates. Hand round salad separately. Serve with granary bread.

FISH DISHES

PLAICE AND MUSHROOM ROLLS *4–6 helpings*

425 ml (¾ pt) semi-skimmed milk
1 bay leaf
2 small sprigs thyme
1 sprig parsley
Salt and pepper
65 g (2½ oz) butter
335 g (12 oz) open cup mushrooms,
  wiped
1 small onion, finely chopped
50 g (2 oz) finely chopped green
  pepper

15 ml (1 tablesp) chopped parsley
30 ml (2 tablesp) fresh breadcrumbs
4–6 plaice fillets
25 g (1 oz) flour
1 egg yolk
Parmesan cheese

GARNISH:
Parsley or thyme

In a covered pan heat, but do not boil, milk with bay leaf, herb sprigs and seasoning. Remove from heat and infuse 10 minutes. Reserve 4 mushrooms for garnish, chop the rest. Heat 40 g (1½ oz) butter in a frying pan and cook the onion, mushrooms and green pepper until tender. Stir in chopped parsley and breadcrumbs. Place fish fillets skin-side uppermost on the table. Season and divide the stuffing evenly between the fillets. Roll them up and arrange in a greased ovenproof dish. Strain the infused milk. Make a white sauce with remaining butter, flour and milk. Remove from heat. Stir in egg yolk and check seasoning. Pour sauce over fish rolls. Sprinkle a little grated Parmesan cheese over. Bake in oven at 200° C, 400° F, Mark 6 for about 6 min. Cook the reserved mushrooms for garnish in a foil parcel in the oven for 15 minutes. Arrange garnish mushrooms on the dish and add 1–2 parsley sprigs, plus a little thyme, if liked.

HAKE WITH ORANGE AND DILL SAUCE *4 helpings*

4 × 175–225 g (6–8 oz) hake steaks
284 ml (½ pt) fish or chicken stock
15 ml (1 tablesp) fresh dill
Salt and freshly ground black pepper
2 oranges, peeled and cut into
  segments

15 ml (1 tablesp) cornflour
85 ml (3 fl oz) concentrated Florida
  orange juice

GARNISH:
Fresh dill

Poach the hake steaks in the stock with the dill and seasoning for 8–10 min. Drain and transfer to a warmed serving dish. Reserve the poaching liquid. Mix the cornflour to a paste with the orange juice. Add to the reserved liquid with the orange segments. Cook, stirring, until mixture is thickened and hot. Spoon some over the fish. Garnish with the fresh dill. Hand round remaining sauce separately.

HERRINGS WITH LEMON AND ROSEMARY *2–4 helpings*

4 herrings, filleted
25 g (1 oz) seasoned flour
15 g (½ oz) butter or margarine
15 ml (1 tablesp) sunflower oil

5 ml (1 teasp) dried rosemary
15 ml (1 tablesp) lemon juice

GARNISH:
Lemon wedges

Dust the fillets in seasoned flour. Heat butter and oil in a large frying pan. Add rosemary and lemon juice, then add the fillets. Cook for 2 min on each side. Serve piping hot garnished with lemon wedges.

Herrings with lemon and rosemary.

Plaice with mushroom rolls.

Hake with orange and dill sauce.

SCALLOP KEBABS *4 helpings*

6 fresh scallops, sliced in half
8 whole prawns
1 large red pepper, de-seeded
1 large green pepper, de-seeded

MARINADE:
142 ml (¼ pt) oil

5 ml (1 teasp) fennel seeds
10 ml (2 teasp) chopped fresh basil
10 ml (2 teasp) chopped fresh chervil
2 bay leaves
30 ml (2 tablesp) lemon juice
Salt and freshly ground black pepper

With a small sweet or cocktail cutter cut 8 circles from each pepper. Starting and ending with a piece of pepper, thread scallops, prawns and peppers on to 4 skewers. Lay in a shallow dish. Put all the ingredients for the marinade into a container with a lid (screw-top jar is ideal) and shake to mix well. Pour over kebabs. Cover and refrigerate for 1½–2 hours. Grill or barbecue for 5–10 min, turning once. Serve accompanied with brown or white rice.

RED MULLET WITH TOMATO SAUCE *4 helpings*

4 red mullet
45 ml (3 tablesp) oil
5 ml (1 teasp) paprika
10 ml (2 teasp) tomato chutney
175 ml (6 fl oz) skinned tomato pulp

1 bay leaf
Pinch basil
Sprig of thyme
Salt and pepper

GARNISH:
Lemon wedges

Heat oil and add paprika, chutney, tomato pulp, bay leaf and basil. Simmer for 3 min. Clean mullet and lay in an ovenproof dish. Add thyme and season fish well. Spoon sauce over. Cook at 180°C, 350°F, Mark 4, for about 20 min, basting occasionally. Serve hot or cold garnished with lemon wedges.

TROUT WITH FENNEL SAUCE *2 helpings*

2 farm trout, cleaned and gutted

SAUCE:
142 ml (¼ pt) soured cream

5 ml (1 teasp) lemon juice
5 ml (1 teasp) chopped fresh fennel or
¼ teasp dried fennel powder
Salt and freshly ground black pepper

Place fish in a lightly greased ovenproof dish and cover with greased greaseproof paper or wrap in buttered foil. Cook in the oven at 180° C, 350° F, Mark 4, for about 20 min. To make the sauce, mix the soured cream with the lemon juice, fennel and seasoning. Heat gently over a moderate heat, but do not allow sauce to boil. Arrange fish on warmed serving plates and pour sauce over.

MEAT DISHES

LIVER WITH HERBY BREADCRUMBS *3–4 helpings*

6 thin slices lamb's liver
45 ml (3 tablesp) flour
2 eggs, beaten

HERBY BREADCRUMBS:
100 g (4 oz) fresh breadcrumbs
½ teasp each dried rosemary, sage, tarragon
Salt and black pepper
Oil for shallow frying

Skin and trim liver if necessary. Mix breadcrumbs with herbs and seasoning. Coat liver in flour, dip in egg and finally coat in breadcrumb mixture. Press crumbs on firmly. Heat oil in a pan and fry liver until coating is golden and crisp (about 10 min). Serve with a spicy sauce and a selection of green vegetables.

VALENTINE LAMB WITH TARRAGON *4 helpings*

4–8 boneless loin lamb steaks
Salt and pepper
10 ml (2 teasp) oil
15 g (½ oz) butter

SAUCE:
25 g (1 oz) butter

60 ml (4 tablesp) Madeira or *sweet sherry*
15 ml (1 tablesp) finely chopped fresh tarragon
45 ml (3 tablesp) double cream

GARNISH:
Tarragon sprigs

Season the meat. Heat oil and butter. Brown meat for 5–10 min each side. Arrange on a serving dish and keep warm. Make the sauce: Add the butter, Madeira or sweet sherry, tarragon and cream to the pan and heat, but do not boil. Pour over the meat and serve immediately garnished with tarragon sprigs.

PICNIC PASTIES *Makes 6*

*335 g (12 oz) made-weight
  wholemeal pastry*
*675 g (1½ lb) low-fat pork
  sausagemeat*
5 ml (1 teasp) dried mixed herbs
5 ml (1 teasp) chopped chervil
30 ml (2 tablesp) grated onion
Salt and pepper to taste

Wholegrain mustard
A little flour
6 hard-boiled eggs
1 egg, beaten

GARNISH:
Chervil or parsley

Pre-heat oven at 200° C, 400° F, Mark 6. Mix sausagemeat with herbs, onion and seasoning. Roll out pastry thinly and cut into 6 pieces, each 23 cm (9 in) long and 15 cm (6 in) wide. Spread wholegrain mustard over pastry but leave a 1.5 cm (¾ in) edge. Divide sausagemeat into 6 and use completely to cover each egg (easier if the egg is rolled in a little flour first). Lay a covered egg in centre of each pastry strip, brush edges with beaten egg, then bring the 2 narrow ends together over the egg and seal. Thoroughly seal side edges. Crimp attractively. Brush pasties with beaten egg to glaze. Cook, towards top of oven, for 15 min, then reduce heat to 180° C, 350° F, Mark 4, and continue cooking for a further 30–40 min, or until cooked through. Eat cold.

BARBECUE BURGERS *Makes 6*

450 g (1 lb) finely minced lean beef
or pork or lamb
1 onion, minced or finely chopped
20 ml (1 tablesp plus 1 teasp) white
or brown breadcrumbs

1 egg
Salt and pepper
Flavourings (see below)

Mix basic ingredients together in a large bowl. Add suitable flavourings. Divide the shape into 6 burgers. When charcoal has become ashen-grey and glowing hot, cook for 10 min each side.

FLAVOURINGS:

Beef
30 ml (2 tablesp) horseradish sauce
½ teasp grated horseradish

Pork
5 ml (1 teasp) chopped fresh sage
or
½ teasp dried sage

Lamb
15 ml (1 tablesp) rosemary
or
5 ml (1 teasp) coriander

Valentine lamb with tarragon.

Liver with herby breadcrumbs.

POULTRY DISHES

SAFFRON GLAZED CHICKEN
WITH HERBED SWEETCORN *4 helpings*

4 chicken joints
¼ teasp saffron strands
45 ml (3 tablesp) dry white wine
30 ml (2 tablesp) oil
Salt and freshly ground black pepper
A little oil or melted butter for
  cooking
1 × 335 g (11.8 oz) can sweetcorn
  kernels
25 g (1 oz) butter

15 ml (1 tablesp) chopped fresh
  tarragon

GARNISH:
Sprigs of tarragon

Make a few small cuts in each chicken joint and place them in a shallow ovenproof dish. Mix saffron strands with the wine. Heat gently in a saucepan. Stir in the oil and brush mixture evenly over chicken portion. Cover. Chill for 2 hours. Brush chicken once again with any remaining saffron marinade. Season and arrange them, flesh side uppermost, in the dish. Brush with a little oil or melted butter and cook in the oven at 190° C, 375° F, Mark 5, for about 40 min or until just tender. For the sweetcorn: Drain sweetcorn and heat through in a pan with butter, chopped tarragon and seasoning to taste. Serve the herbed sweetcorn around the chicken. Garnish with tarragon sprigs.

MUSHROOM AND TURKEY KORMA *4 helpings*

284 ml (½ pt) natural yogurt
3 dried red chillis, finely ground
½ teasp each: ground coriander and
  ground ginger
6 cardomoms, ground
3 bay leaves
Freshly milled black pepper

800 g (1 lb 12 oz) turkey casserole
  meat
30 ml (2 tablesp) oil
2 onions, cut lengthwise into slices
100 g (4 oz) button mushrooms,
  wiped
2 cloves garlic, crushed
142 ml (¼ pt) chicken stock
15 ml (1 tablesp) lemon juice

Place yogurt in a basin. Stir in prepared spices, bay leaves and seasoning. Add turkey and leave on one side. Heat oil, brown onions, then stir in mushrooms and garlic. Cook for 2 min. Add turkey with yogurt and stock. Bring to boil. Cover. Simmer for about 1¼ hours. Stir in lemon juice, then boil rapidly to reduce liquor. Serve accompanied by a crisp salad.

WHOLE CHICKEN WITH LOBSTER *6 helpings*

100 g (4 oz) cream cheese
1 clove garlic, crushed
Salt and freshly ground black pepper
15 ml (1 tablesp) chopped fresh dill
100 g (4 oz) flaked cooked lobster
  meat (the pinker the better)

40 g (1½ oz) butter
4 large lettuce leaves or Chinese
  leaves
200 ml (⅓ pt) dry white wine
1.5 kg (3½ lb) chicken, prepared for
  cooking

Mix cream cheese with the garlic, seasoning, dill and flaked lobster. Place the chicken on a board, breast side uppermost. Carefully ease your fingers from one end of the bird to the other, separating the skin from the flesh. Ease the flavoured cream cheese evenly between the skin and the chicken flesh, making sure that you do not pierce the skin. Place the 'stuffed' chicken in a roasting tin and dot with butter; season and cover with lettuce leaves. Spoon over white wine and cover with a piece of foil. Roast in oven at 190°C, 375°F, Mark 5, for 1½ – 1¾ hours or until tender.

SAVOURY AND EGG DISHES

EGGS WITH HERBY CUCUMBER AND HERBY DRESSING *4 helpings*

6 hard-boiled eggs

DRESSING:
About 225 g (8 oz) natural yogurt
1 clove garlic, crushed
15 ml (1 tablesp) chopped fresh
  tarragon or mint or parsley
15 ml (1 tablesp) chopped Florence
  fennel

Salt and pepper
1 cucumber, coarsely grated

GARNISH:
Cucumber slices
Radishes
1 hard-boiled egg, sliced

Liquidise yogurt with garlic, herb of choice and fennel. Season to taste.

Saffron glazed chicken.

Eggs with herby dressing.

Cover and chill. Put grated cucumber into a sieve and strain for 30 min. Turn into yogurt mixture and stir well. Halve 6 eggs lengthways. Arrange in 3 rows in a dish. Spoon some of the dressing over centre row. Garnish dish with cucumber slices, radishes, sliced egg. Hand round remaining dressing separately.

NB. This dressing goes well with green salads, curry and with cold fish. Herbs can be mixed to suit personal taste.

HUMMOS *6 helpings*

175 – 225 g (6 – 8 oz) chick peas,
*   soaked overnight*
2 – 3 cloves garlic, crushed (or to
*   taste)*
15 ml (1 tablesp) tahina
Juice of 2 lemons
45 – 60 ml (3 – 4 tablesp) olive oil
*   (or to taste)*

Salt
Pinch cumin or a little chopped mint

GARNISH:
Chopped parsley

Cook chick peas in fresh water until very soft. Drain and cool. Blend all ingredients, except olive oil, until smooth. Alternatively pass chick peas and garlic through a mouli while still warm, add tahina, lemon juice, salt and herb. Stir in olive oil to taste. Serve either chilled or at room temperature, with a generous sprinkling of parsley over. Accompany with hot pitta bread. Can be served as a starter, an appetiser, a snack or as an accompaniment to kebabs.

CLASSIC OMELET
AUX FINES HERBES *1 helping*

3 eggs
15 ml (3 tablesp) cold water
Salt and freshly ground black pepper

15 ml (1 tablesp) chopped mixed
*   parsley, chives, tarragon and*
*   chervil*
15 g (½ oz) butter

Break eggs into a bowl, add water, salt, pepper and herbs and beat lightly to break up whites and yolks. Heat a 15 – 18 cm (6 – 7 in) omelette pan gently, add butter and turn up heat. As soon as butter sizzles (take care it does not brown), pour in eggs. With a fork or spatula draw cooked egg from edge of pan towards the centre so that the liquid egg runs to base of pan and cooks. While the top is still slightly runny, fold over ⅓ of the omelette away from pan handle. Remove from heat. To turn out, hold handle of pan with palm of hand uppermost, shake the omelette to the edge of pan and tip pan completely over on to a warm serving plate, so making another fold.

NB. Many mixtures can be added to a basic omelette, such as mixed chives, parsley, thyme, marjoram; or equal quantities of chervil and mint or coriander and chives.

EGG AND HORSERADISH TOASTIES *4–8 helpings*

*15 ml (1 tablesp) grated horseradish
  (or to taste)
15 ml (1 tablesp) chopped chives*

*175 g (6 oz) cream cheese or
  medium-fat soft cheese
8 slices bread for toasting
8 eggs*

Blend horseradish and chives into the cheese. Toast the bread and spread with the mixture. Meanwhile poach the eggs. Place toast under a medium-hot grill for about 30 seconds, serve each slice topped with an egg.

SAVOURY RICE *4 helpings*

*175 g (6 oz) brown, unpolished rice
10 ml (2 teasp) chopped mixed fresh
  herbs of choice
2 large carrots, grated
1 onion, finely chopped*

*15 ml (1 tablesp) chopped red or
  green pepper
Chicken stock or white vegetable
  stock
175–225 g (6–8 oz) mature Cheddar
  cheese, grated*

Thoroughly wash the rice. Place in a saucepan. Add carrots, onion, herbs and pepper. Cover with boiling chicken stock or well-seasoned vegetable stock. Put lid on pan and cook, adding a little more stock if necessary, until rice is tender (about 50 min). The rice should be soft and separate and the liquid absorbed. Turn into a warmed serving dish and cover liberally with the cheese.

NB. The cheese can be omitted and the rice served on its own or as an accompaniment to any savoury dish.

MID-WEEK PIE *3–4 helpings*

275 g (10 oz) Double Gloucester
  cheese, grated
75 g (3 oz) day-old wholemeal
  breadcrumbs
50 g (2 oz) butter or margarine
1 cucumber, peeled and thinly sliced
1 onion, grated
Salt and pepper

1 clove garlic, crushed
225 g (8 oz) tomatoes, roughly
  chopped
5 ml (1 teasp) chervil or basil or
  oregano

GARNISH:
Chervil or watercress

Mix 50 g (2 oz) of the cheese with the breadcrumbs and set aside. Using some of the butter well-grease a generous 1 ltr (2 pt) ovenproof dish or pie-dish. Spread half remaining cheese over the base. Cover with half cucumber slices and then the onion. Season lightly with salt and pepper. Top with rest of the cheese and then the cucumber. Either liquidise tomatoes with garlic and herbs, or sieve tomatoes and mix with garlic and herbs. Pour into dish. Spread breadcrumb mixture over, season with pepper and dot with rest of butter. Stand dish on a baking sheet and cook, in centre of oven, at 190°C, 375°F, Mark 5, for 1–1¼ hours or until cooked through and the top is browned and crispy. Garnish with chervil or watercress. Eat hot or cold.

SALADS

COURGETTE, APPLE AND LOVAGE SALAD *3–4 helpings*

3 raw courgettes, trimmed and
  shredded or finely sliced
1 eating apple, peeled, cored, grated
50 g (2 oz) raw button mushrooms,
  thinly sliced

DRESSING:
90 ml (6 tablesp) natural yogurt

15 ml (1 tablesp) chopped fresh
  lovage
5 ml (1 teasp) tarragon vinegar or
  lemon juice
Radicchio leaves

GARNISH:
Fresh lovage

Arrange radicchio leaves as a bed on a serving plate. Mix remaining ingredients together and spoon into centre of bed. Garnish with lovage. Serve with cold pork, bacon or cheese.

CRUNCHY SALAD *4 helpings*

657 g (1 lb) new potatoes, boiled
150 ml (¼ pt) thick salad cream or
   mayonnaise
5 ml (1 teasp) curry powder
Salt and white pepper
15 ml (1 tablesp) chopped chives

50 g (2 oz) chopped walnuts
100 g (4 oz) mooli, diced
2 carrots, sliced
175 g (6 oz) Cheddar cheese, cubed

Dice the potatoes while they are still warm. Mix curry powder into salad cream. Add seasoning. Mix in still warm potatoes and leave for 1 hour to allow flavours to blend. Then mix in remaining ingredients. Serve with a green salad.

LITTLE GEM AND PEA SALAD *4 helpings*

2–3 Little Gem lettuces, washed,
   dried, quartered
335 g (12 oz) cold, cooked peas

DRESSING:
30 ml (2 tablesp) wine vinegar

Salt and pepper to taste
½ teasp caster sugar
90 ml (6 tablesp) oil
30 ml (2 tablesp) finely chopped fresh
   mint

To make the dressing: Put vinegar in a basin or large, screw-top jar. Add salt, pepper, sugar, mix well, then add the oil. Either mix well or put lid on container and shake. Add mint and stir or shake again. Toss peas in the dressing. Arrange lettuce quarters on plates and spoon peas in the middle of the quarters with a slatted spoon. Serve with cold roast lamb or cold duck.

BEAN SPROUTS WITH GREEN DRESSING *4–6 helpings*

335 g (12 oz) bean sprouts, rinsed
   and drained

DRESSING:
150 g (5 oz) natural yogurt or soured
   cream or mayonnaise
30 ml (2 tablesp) chopped parsley

15 ml (1 tablesp) chopped tarragon
10 ml (2 teasp) chopped borage
15 ml (1 teasp) chopped chives
5 ml (1 teasp) lemon juice or wine
   vinegar
Salt and pepper to taste

Make dressing by mixing all ingredients together or by liquidising.

Cover and chill for at least 2 hours before serving. Shortly before serving stir in bean sprouts and mix thoroughly.

NB. Other herbs can be used in place of those suggested and other ingredients, such as cubed cheese, can be included with the bean sprouts.

VEGETABLES

RED CABBAGE WITH APPLE AND CARAWAY *4–6 helpings*

1 medium-sized red cabbage, washed,
  drained, shredded
1 Bramley's Seedling apple, peeled,
  cored, chopped
45 ml (3 tablesp) cider vinegar

142 ml (¼ pt) water
½ teasp caraway seeds or to taste, tied
  in muslin bag
Salt and freshly ground black pepper
50 g (2 oz) chopped walnuts

Place all ingredients, except walnuts, into a pan, bring to boil, cover and simmer for 10 min. Add walnuts and re-cover pan. Simmer for another 5 – 10 mins. The cabbage should still be a little crispy. Remove caraway seeds, drain cabbage well and serve piping hot.

SQUARE DANCE POTATOES *4–6 helpings*

675 g (1½ lb) potatoes, scrubbed
and diced
50 g (2 oz) butter
30 ml (2 tablesp) chopped parsley

30 ml (2 tablesp) chopped chives
15 ml (1 tablesp) chopped mint
Salt and pepper

Place potatoes in a pan and cover with cold, lightly salted water. Bring to boil, cover and simmer for about 5 min, or just cooked. Drain well. Wipe out pan. Melt the butter and add herbs and seasoning. Carefully toss the potatoes in the mixture. (Good as an accompaniment to any savoury dish).

NB. Herbs can be any mixture that appeals to you: e.g. add a hint of borage or summer savory, or use chervil in place of parsley.

DORSET POTATOES *4 helpings*

*675 g (1½ lb) smoothly mashed
potatoes
½ bunch watercress
½ teasp chopped fresh savory or a
pinch if dried*

*15 g (½ oz) butter or margarine
Salt and freshly ground black pepper*

Remove any thick stems from the watercress. Finely chop thin stems and the leaves. Beat fat and seasoning, with the savory, into the potatoes and serve piping hot.

SUMMER CARROTS *4 helpings*

*450 g (1 lb) young carrots, scrubbed
15 g (½ oz) butter
5 ml (1 teasp) soft brown sugar
About 300 ml (½ pt) chicken or
white vegetable stock*

*10 ml (2 teasp) each: chopped fresh
mint, rosemary and parsley
15 ml (1 tablesp) lemon or orange
juice
Salt and pepper*

Put young carrots, butter and sugar into a thick-based saucepan, just cover with stock, bring to boil. Simmer, uncovered, on a moderate heat until liquid has been absorbed. Stir in the herbs, lemon or orange juice and the seasoning. Cook for a further 2 min.

CAULIFLOWER CAPRICE *2–3 helpings*

*1 small cauliflower, trimmed and left
whole
A little salt
25 g (1 oz) butter
25 g (1 oz) flour
142 ml (¼ pt) milk
142 ml (¼ pt) cauliflower water (see
method)
Freshly ground black pepper*

*5 ml (1 teasp) marjoram or chervil
2 hard-boiled eggs, finely chopped
50 g (2 oz) medium-fat (curd) cheese
50 g (2 oz) Cheddar cheese, grated*

*GARNISH:
Fresh marjoram or chervil*

Put cauliflower into a pan and pour in sufficient boiling water nearly to cover. Add salt. Cover and simmer for 15 min or until just tender. Drain. Reserve liquid. Keep cauliflower hot. Make a white sauce with butter, flour and milk. Add herb and 142 ml (¼ pt) cauliflower water.

Cook for 1 min, then remove from heat. Add eggs and curd cheese, stir until smooth. Season with pepper to taste. The sauce should be thick but if a thinner sauce is preferred stir in more of the reserved cauliflower liquid. Place the well-drained cauliflower in a warmed heatproof dish. Spoon sauce over. Sprinkle grated cheese on top. Pop under moderately hot grill until cheese has bubbled and turned golden brown. Garnish with marjoram or chervil.

PUDDINGS AND SWEETS

HAREM JELLY *4–6 helpings*

1 pkt orange jelly
425 ml (¾ pt) water
4 eau-de-cologne mint leaves

Bring 284 ml (½ pt) water to the boil, pour over mint leaves, and leave until cold. Strain. Make up jelly using remaining water. Add mint-flavoured water, pour into wetted mould. Turn out when set.

VERBENA CUSTARD *4–5 helpings*

3 – 4 verbena leaves
5 ml (1 teasp) grated lemon rind
568 ml (1 pt) milk

4 eggs
Sugar to taste

Add lemon rind and verbena leaves to the milk. Cover and leave to infuse for 30 min. Meanwhile pre-heat oven at 170°C, 325°F, Mark 3. Strain milk into a pan, heat, but do not boil. Lightly whisk eggs with the sugar and, stirring, pour hot milk over. Strain mixture into a greased ovenproof dish. Stand in a baking tin. Fill tin about 2.5 cm (1 in) deep with warm water and bake, in centre of oven, for approximately 45 min, or until custard is firm to the touch and set. Eat hot or cold.

STRAWBERRIES WITH . . .

Firm, ripe strawberries
Accompaniments:

CREAM WITH CRÈME DE MENTHE

142 ml (¼ pt) fresh double cream
10 ml (2 teasp) icing sugar
20 ml (4 teasp) Crème de Menthe

GARNISH:
Sprigs of fresh mint

Whisk the cream until it thickens slightly and gradually fold in remaining ingredients. Garnish with fresh mint.

MINT DIP

142 ml (¼ pt) bottle of mint syrup
   (sweetened)
10 ml (2 teasp) finely chopped fresh
   mint

Mix ingredients together. (A different kind of mint, such as pineapple mint can be used for this recipe)

YOGURT WITH MINT

150 g (5 oz) natural yogurt
Icing sugar to taste

10 ml (2 teasp) finely chopped fresh
   mint
Mint syrup or Crème de Menthe to
   taste

Mix ingredients thoroughly and infuse in a cool place for at least 1 hour.

WESTMORLAND MINTY PASTY 6 helpings

Rich short pastry:
225 g (8 oz) self-raising flour sifted
   with a pinch of salt
125 g (5 oz) margarine
15 g (½ oz) sugar
Water to mix

FILLING:
50 g (2 oz) butter
50 g (2 oz) soft brown sugar
100 g (4 oz) currants
40 ml (2½ tablesp) chopped fresh
   mint
Water
Caster sugar

Pre-heat oven at 200°C, 400°F, Mark 6. Rub fat into flour until the breadcrumb stage. Mix in sugar and then sufficient water to make a firm dough. Turn out on to a floured board. Divide pastry into 2 and roll each piece into a square. Leave in a cool place while you prepare the filling. Cream butter and sugar, stir in currants and mint and mix throughly. Place 1 pastry square on a baking sheet. Brush round edges with water. Spread currant filling evenly in the middle. Top with second pastry square. Seal edges and crimp decoratively. Cut 3 – 4 slits in the top. Brush with water and sprinkle caster sugar over. Bake just above centre of oven for 20 – 25 min.

SCENTED PEARS *4 helpings*

4 cooking pears, whole but peeled and   *2 sprigs eau-de-cologne mint*
  cored   *Brown sugar to taste*
Ginger ale or water

Put pears in a saucepan. Half cover with ginger ale or water. Add mint and sugar. Bring to boil, cover and simmer until pears are tender but not turning mushy. Remove mint. Leave pears to get cold. Serve with a little of the cooking liquid poured over.

CAKES, BISCUITS AND BREAD

HERBED CHEESE BREAD

1 long French loaf   *15 ml (1 tablesp) chopped fresh mixed*
100 g (4 oz) butter, softened   *herbs*
75 g (3 oz) grated cheese   or
                                               5 ml (1 teasp) dried mixed herbs

Pre-heat oven at 200°C, 400°F, Mark 6. Make 11 cuts along the bread to within 1 cm (½ in) of the base. Open up slightly. Mash together the butter, cheese and herbs to mix them thoroughly. Generously spread into each side of the cuts of bread. Wrap the loaf tightly in foil. Bake for about 30 min. Unwrap and serve hot.

GARLIC BREAD

1 French loaf   *Creamed butter as required*
2 – 3 cloves garlic, crushed

Cut loaf crosswise, taking care not to cut through final crust. Then treat like herbed cheese bread. Unwrap and serve hot.

PEASANT BREAD

About 850 ml (1½ pt) water   *25 g (1 oz) salt*
25 g (1 oz) dried yeast   *50 g (2 oz) lard*
900 g (2 lb) wholemeal flour   *15 ml (1 tablesp) fennel seeds*
450 g (1 lb) plain white flour   *25 g (1 oz) sugar*

Warm 142 ml (¼ pt) of the water to blood heat. Sprinkle in the yeast, whisk lightly, leave in warm place for 10–15 min, until yeast has dissolved and top is bubbly. Mix the flours and salt together. Rub in the fat. Stir in seeds and sugar. Make a well in the middle, pour in yeast mixture and most of the water. Stir until a soft dough is formed, adding a little more water if required. Knead until smooth, leave to rise until doubled in size. Meanwhile, grease 450 g (1 lb) loaf tins, then dust them with flour. Turn dough on to lightly-floured board. Knead and put into tins. Leave to prove until tins are full. Bake near top of oven at 230°C, 450°F, Mark 8 for 15 min, reduce heat to 200°C, 400°F, Mark 6 and cook for a further 40 – 50 min, or until loaves sound 'hollow'.

CARAWAY BISCUITS *Yield approximately 24 biscuits*

225 g (8 oz) flour   *75 g (3 oz) caster sugar*
Pinch of salt   *5 ml (1 teasp) caraway seeds*
½ teasp cinnamon   *1 large egg yolk*
75 g (3 oz) butter   *Egg and caster sugar to sprinkle over*

Pre-heat oven 190°C, 375°F, Mark 5. Sift flour, salt and cinnamon into a bowl, rub in the fat, stir in sugar and seeds. Add beaten egg yolk and knead well. Roll out into ½ cm (¼ in) thick rounds, brush with a little beaten egg, sprinkle sugar over and bake over centre of oven for 10 – 15 min.

SAVOURY BISCUITS *Yield 15–18 biscuits*

75 g (3 oz) plain flour
50 g (2 oz) fine oatmeal
½ teasp dry mixed herbs or 1 teasp
  chopped fresh herbs

Salt and pepper
50 g (2 oz) margarine or butter
50 g (2 oz) grated Cheddar cheese
1 egg, lightly beaten

Pre-heat oven at 190°C, 375°F, Mark 5. Mix flour, oats, seasoning and herbs in a basin, rub in fat, stir in cheese. Add sufficient egg to make a firm dough. Roll out thinly on a floured board, use a 7.5 cm (3 in) cutter to make the biscuits. Place on lightly-greased baking sheet. Brush over with remaining egg. Cook in centre of oven for about 15 min. Cool on wire tray.

RICH SEED CAKE

225 g (8 oz) self-raising flour
½ teasp cinnamon
Pinch nutmeg (or to taste)
10 ml (2 teasp) caraway seeds

175 g (6 oz) butter or margarine
175 g (6 oz) caster sugar
3 eggs, beaten
Milk to mix

Pre-heat oven at 180°C, 350°F, Mark 4. Line a greased 17.5 cm (7 in) cake tin with greased greaseproof paper. Sieve together flour, cinnamon and nutmeg. Stir in caraway seeds. Cream butter with sugar until light and fluffy, beat in the eggs a little at a time, then fold in flour. Add sufficient milk to make a soft dropping consistency. Bake just below centre of oven for 1 – 1¼ hours, or until cooked through.

SAUCES AND DRESSINGS

PROVENÇAL SAUCE

1 onion, finely chopped
30 ml (2 tablesp) oil
200 g (8 oz) can tomatoes
15 ml (1 tablesp) tomato purée

½ teasp dried basil or oregano or
rosemary
1 clove garlic, crushed
Pinch caster sugar
Salt and pepper

Fry onion gently in oil for 5 min. Add remaining ingredients. Simmer 5 min. (Good with sausages, barbecued meats and poached fish).

DILLY APPLE SAUCE

450 g (1 lb) cooking apples, peeled,
  cored and sliced
30 ml (2 tablesp) water

15 – 25 g (½ – 1 oz) sugar
A small knob of butter or margarine
10 ml (2 teasp) freshly-chopped dill

Cook apples with water over gentle heat until soft and dry, add sugar and butter, beat or sieve until smooth and stir in the dill. Serve hot or cold. This sauce makes an easy filling for an omelet.

ELIZABETHAN SAUCE FOR PORK

675 g (1½ lb) cooking apples,
  peeled, cored and sliced
225 g (8 oz) quince, peeled, cored
  and sliced
30 – 45 ml (2 – 3 tablesp) water

Juice of 1 lemon
25 – 50 g (1 – 2 oz) sugar
50 g (2 oz) butter
20 ml (4 teasp) freshly-chopped mint

Put apples, quince, water, lemon juice and sugar in a pan, simmer until soft and dry, taking care the mixture does not burn. Stir in butter, heat or sieve until smooth, then add the mint. Re-heat very gently, if necessary. (Very good with bacon, sausages and goose as well as pork.)

LEEK AND HERB SAUCE

About 225 g (8 oz) thinly sliced
  leeks, including green tops
284 ml (½ pt) water
¼ teasp dried rosemary or

5 ml (1 teasp) finely chopped mint
25 g (1 oz) butter or margarine
25 g (1 oz) flour
142 ml (¼ pt) fresh double cream

Simmer leeks, with the herb, in the water until tender (about 10 min). Cool a little, then liquidise. Make a roux with the butter and flour, then carefully stir in the leek purée to make a smooth mixture. Bring to boil, stirring. Cook for 1 min. Add cream and bring to just under boiling point. To serve, spoon a little over grilled lamb or steak, or hot boiled bacon, and hand round remaining sauce separately.
NB. You can use other herbs for this sauce; e.g. chopped fennel to serve with fish.

QUICK HORSERADISH SAUCE

60 ml (4 tablesp) natural yogurt
60 ml (4 tablesp) soured cream or
  salad cream
30 – 45 ml (2 – 3 tablesp) grated
  horseradish

White wine vinegar to taste
Salt and white pepper

Lightly whip yogurt with soured cream or salad dressing. Stir in remaining ingredients. Cover. Refrigerate for at least 1 hour before serving. Use within 24 hours.

MINT SAUCE

Mint sprigs, washed and dried
Sugar

Boiling water
White or malt vinegar

Discard any coarse, thick mint stems. Place selected mint on a board and sprinkle a little sugar over. Chop finely (the sugar not only helps make chopping easier but also absorbs oils from the mint). To every 30 ml (2 level tablesp) chopped mint allow 15 ml (1 tablsp) boiling water and ½ teasp sugar (or to taste). Stir to dissolve sugar. Pour in vinegar to taste and leave to infuse for at least 1 hour before serving.

PARSLEY SAUCE

284 ml (½ pt) freshly made white
  sauce
Salt and pepper

15 ml (1 tablesp) chopped parsley

As soon as the sauce is ready, season well, remove from heat. Stir in parsley and serve piping hot. Good with broad beans, boiled bacon and baked beetroot.

STUFFINGS AND SUNDRIES

PARSLEY AND THYME DUMPLINGS

100 g (4 oz) self-raising flour
Salt and pepper to taste
50 g (2 oz) shredded suet

15 ml (1 tablesp) chopped parsley
½ teasp dried thyme (or herb of
choice)
Cold water to mix

Sieve flour with salt and pepper. Add suet, parsley and thyme. Mix to a soft but firm dough with cold water. Form into 8 small balls with floured hands. Add to soup or stew for final 20 min cooking time.

PARSLEY AND THYME STUFFING

100 g (4 oz) fresh white breadcrumbs
25 g (1 oz) shredded suet or butter,
grated
15 ml (1 tablesp) chopped parsley
10 ml (2 teasp) chopped thyme

Finely-grated rind of ½ lemon
Salt and pepper
1 egg, beaten
Milk to bind

Mix together all the ingredients, using sufficient milk to bind.

SAGE AND ONION STUFFING

4 onions, sliced
7 fresh sage leaves or 1 level dessertsp
powdered sage
25 g (1 oz) butter

Pepper and salt
100 g (4 oz) soft breadcrumbs
Egg to bind

Simmer the onion in a little water until tender, drain and chop. Add the sage, butter, seasoning, breadcrumbs and leave to cool. Mix in sufficient beaten egg to bind.

STUFFING FOR VEAL

75 g (3 oz) lean ham, minced or
  finely chopped
10 ml (2 teasp) chopped parsley
5 ml (1 teasp) chopped lemon thyme
  or lemon verbena (pinch of finely
  powdered if dried)

A pinch of marjoram
100 g (4 oz) shredded suet
Salt and pepper
175 g (6 oz) soft white breadcrumbs
2 eggs, lightly beaten

Mix first ingredients. Use sufficient egg to bind.

HERB TEAS

There can be a bit of confusion about herb teas. Basically, they are like any other tea, only made with a herb of your choice. Sometimes they are known as Tisanes. They are also referred to as infusions. The latter more often implies that the tea is being regarded not just as a refreshing drink but is used for medicinal purposes or as an aid to beauty (see Chapter 6).

Drink herb tea as you would Indian or China tea, with or without milk, with or without lemon, with or without sweetening. Starting the day with herb tea or having one as a relaxing night-cap can be very soothing.

Always use a china or glass container when making a herb tea. Keep it covered while the tea is brewing. Trial and error will show which herbs you prefer and how much herb in the pot suits your taste. To begin with use 15 ml (3 teasp) freshly-chopped or 5 ml (1 teasp) dried herb for each 600 ml (1 pt) boiling water. Infuse 5 – 10 min. When using seeds, crush or pound them, and add 15 ml (1 tablesp) seeds per 600 ml (1 pt) boiling water. When using spoon measurements they should be level-filled.

BALM TEA 3–4 helpings

25 g (1 oz) freshly chopped lemon
  balm
568 ml (1 pt) boiling water

Sugar or sweetener (optional)
Skimmed milk (optional)

Pour water over lemon balm and leave to infuse for 15 min. Serve with sugar and milk.

CHAMOMILE TEA *1–2 helpings*

*10 – 12 chamomile flowers, less if
   dried*

*600 ml (1 pt) boiling water
Demerara sugar to taste*

Cover flowers with boiling water, infuse 5 min, sweeten. Strain.

ICED MINT TEA *4 helpings*

*1 ltr (1¾ pt) cold, made tea (China
   or Indian)
4 thin slices each: lemon and orange
   rind
Crushed ice*

*6 crushed mint leaves
Sugar or liquid sweetner (optional)*

*GARNISH
Lemon slices and mint leaves*

Put crushed ice into base of 4 glasses. Pour tea over. Add orange and
lemon rind and 1½ mint leaves to each. Sweeten if desired. Serve
garnished with lemon slices and mint leaves.

OSWEGO TEA

*20 ml (4 teasp) freshly-chopped
   bergamot
568 ml (1 pt) boiling water*

Sugar or honey to taste

Pour water over chopped leaves, infuse for 5 – 10 min, strain, sweeten
and serve.

DRINKS

CLARET CUP (Alcoholic) *8–10 helpings*

*8 thin slices lemon
12 thin slices cucumber
1 large bottle soda-water
1 wine glass brandy*

*1 bottle claret
50 g (2 oz) sugar or liquid sweetener
   to taste
3 sprigs borage
Ice cubes*

Put first 6 ingredients into a large jug. Stir with a long spoon until sugar
has dissolved, then stir in borage. Cover. Refrigerate for 1 – 2 hours.
Strain. Add ice cubes.

CITRUS CUP 5–7 *helpings*

284 ml (½ pt) grapefruit juice
425 ml (¾ pt) unsweetened orange
  juice
142 ml (¼ pt) lemon juice
425 ml (¾ pt) water
Sugar or sweetener to taste (optional)

6 – 8 mint leaves, slightly crushed
  (pineapple mint best)

GARNISH:
Mint leaves or borage flowers

Mix fruit juices, water and sugar, stir until sugar has dissolved. Add remaining ingredients. Serve chilled, decorated with mint leaves or borage flowers.

YOGURT AND MINT COOLER 2 *helpings*

300 ml (½ pt) natural yogurt (goat's
  yogurt is good for this)
300 ml (½ pt) cold water or
  skimmed milk

A pinch of salt
10 ml (2 teasp) dried mint (or to
  taste)

Chill yogurt and milk well then liquidise all ingredients. Serve immediately while ice cold. Ice cubes can be added if liked.

BORAGE CUP (Alcoholic) 4–5 *helpings*

600 ml (1 pt) cider
About 300 ml (½ pt) soda-water
Peel of ¼ cucumber
Thinly-pared skin of ½ lemon
1 sprig borage

2 liqueur glasses maraschino
1 liqueur glass brandy
Sugar to taste
Ice
Borage for decoration

Slightly crush the borage and mix all the ingredients in a jug, stirring until sugar has dissolved. Leave to blend for about an hour. Strain. Serve with ice and garnish with sprigs of borage.

CHAPTER 6

HERBS FOR BEAUTY AND HEALTH

Throughout the ages and all over the world women have tried to be as beautiful as possible. Herbs have been used to improve and even colour hair, whiten teeth, strengthen gums, brighten and soothe eyes, cleanse the skin, remove freckles and spots, get rid of wrinkles and relieve aching limbs, as well as to alleviate headaches, menstrual pains and minor ailments. Now there is a revival of interest in these time-tested methods which are easy to prepare and light on the purse.

Basically, what are needed most of the time are infusions (that is a standard herb tea, left to brew and then strained) or a herb oil.

To make a herb oil you need 50 g (2 oz) of finely-crushed herbs of choice (you can pound them or put them through a blender), 225 ml (8 fl oz) corn or olive oil, 15 ml (1 tablesp) wine vinegar. Place herbs in a bottle or glass jar, pour oil and vinegar over and leave in the sun or a warm room for two weeks, strain through muslin, squeeze any oil out of the herbs and discard them; process as many times as is needed to get the oil to the strength when it smells strongly of the herbs. A good test is to rub a little on the back of your hand. Lavender, fennel, rosemary, tarragon are very good herbs to use. Try to gather the herbs (leaf part only, unless you use seeds for a special mixture) in the summer. For decoration add a sprig of dried herb to the final jar. Make a selection of oils, some for beauty, some to add to salad dressings and some for other uses.

Hair is said to be a woman's crowning glory. Make it so for you. Rosemary, chamomile and sage are recommended for hair itself; parsley for the scalp.

If you are a brunette, pour a rosemary infusion over your hair; you can use fresh or dried leaves for the final rinse. This will add lustre and a delicate perfume. Blondes should use a chamomile infusion, and for black hair a sage one is best. Rosemary oil is good for dry hair. If the hair is particularly dry, as for instance when you have been sunbathing overlong with your head uncovered, massage oil into head 15 minutes before shampooing.

A clear skin is a boon. A daily drink of parsley tea is an old way of ensuring a healthy skin. A good cold cream helps too, Gently warm up in a pan an unscented cold cream, add a little herb oil of your choice, re-pot, leave to get cold; apply nightly.

To get rid of unsightly spots apply an infusion of sorrel or tansy on cotton wool. To remove freckles, mix one rounded tablespoon grated horseradish with one teacup milk, bring to boiling point, strain and cool. Apply to face with cotton wool, leave to dry, rinse off with tepid water after ten minutes. Repeat every other day as long as is required, making fresh lotion as necessary.

A face pack is not a modern invention; mixed herb leaves, boiled in a little water, mashed, cooled and applied to the face have been used for centuries. Another mask is made with white of egg mixed with a little lemon juice and finely-chopped fennel leaves. Smooth over face, avoiding eyes and mouth, let dry, leave on 15 minutes, rinse off with tepid water.

The water in which you rinse your face has also been considered important by women over the years. Recommended rinses are strained rosemary or lemon balm infusions, cold or warmed up just before using, and left to dry on the face.

Tired or dull eyes mar beauty. An infusion of lemon verbena, carefully strained and cooled and applied in an eye bath, works wonders.

A stye on the eye is painful as well as ugly. An old cure is to apply an infusion of tansy to the sore morning and night. For a black eye (should such ill fortune come your way), or for a bruise, press on crushed hyssop leaves.

A relaxing bath can soothe away aches and pains. Add a little of your favourite herb oil and try out different ones, such as bergamot, to maintain a smooth skin.

Infusions can be added to bath water or fresh or dried herbs can be tied in a bag and held under the hot tap as the water runs in. A bag of marjoram is said to relieve stiffness and rheumatic pains. Fennel infusion or oil is an ancient slimming method. Sprigs of rosemary or lavender, or chamomile (flowers too), are believed to be calming after a busy day, and mint in the bath is held to be invigorating. An infusion should be plentiful and strong: make it about 100 g (4 oz) leaves and 2 litres (3½ pts) water.

Depending a great deal on how badly your feet ache and if you are alone or not, here is a remedy for badly aching feet. Rub the soles and heels with garlic cloves, sit with your feet up for a while and then rinse them in cool water.

Beautiful teeth are an asset; running sage leaves over teeth and your gums is the herbal way of keeping teeth white and gums strong.

Just as herbs have long been valued for home-made beauty preparations, so they have been for medicinal purposes. But don't try to prescribe for yourself or for friends. In case of any possible or definite serious complaint, seek expert advice.

Infusions (teas) are usually taken for minor troubles.

Here are just a few of the well-known herbal remedies. When not taken as a 'tea', take in wineglassfuls, three times a day, either warmed up or cold.

ANGELICA: Heartburn: 15 g (½ oz) dried or 30 g (1 oz) fresh leaves and young stems, with 600 ml (1 pt) boiling water. Take 60 ml (4 tablesp) at a time. A longer drink is a pick-me-up and can also refresh when suffering from a cold.

BASIL: Travel sickness; nausea: 15–30 g (½–1oz) dried leaves per 600 ml (1 pt) boiling water. Take a sherry glass full before retiring.

BAY: Sleeplessness: Put 1 or 2 bay leaves under your pillow.

BERGAMOT: Catarrh: Inhale vapour from infusion of 30 g (1 oz) freshly chopped leaves per 600 ml (1 pt) boiling water.

BORAGE: Beneficial to kidneys; diuretic: Infusion as basil.

SALAD BURNET: Cools blood; helps clear skin: Eat raw leaves or drink infusion as basil. External application of cold infusion helps ease sunburn.

CHAMOMILE: Headaches; sleeplessness; mild tranquiliser: For headaches drink tea (see Teas). For sleeplessness drink tea last thing at night. A cup of warm chamomile tea, sweetened with honey, relieves tiredness and is a mild tranquiliser.

CHERVIL: Tonic; good for memory: About 15 g (½ oz) dried leaves per 600 ml (1 pt) boiling water. Use more herb when infusing fresh leaves.

CORIANDER: Make an infusion with 5 ml (1 teasp) dried leaves or generous pinch seeds per teacup of boiling water.

DILL: Flatulence: 10 ml (2 teasp) pounded seeds per breakfast cup boiling water.

FENNEL: Nerves; cough; tonic: Slightly bruise seeds then infuse as dill for coughs. Use 30 g (1 oz) fresh leaves per 600 ml (1 pt) boiling water as calming tonic.

GARLIC:
Believed to be good for pretty nearly everything: Eat raw for colds and chest complaints. It is known that garlic contains an antibiotic and also has antiseptic properties.

HYSSOP:
Catarrh; tranquiliser: For catarrh use 30 g (1 oz) fresh young tops in standard infusion. For calming the nerves infuse 5 ml (1 teasp) dried flowers per 600 ml (1 pt) boiling water, sweetended with honey.

LEMON BALM:
Soothing nerves; sleeplessness: Eat raw, or drink infusion for nerves; drink tea last thing at night for sleeplessness. (see. Teas).

LOVAGE:
Relieves menstrual strain: 15 ml (3 teasp) fresh leaves, or 10 ml (2 teasp) dried per 600 ml (1 pt) boiling water.

MARJORAM:
For nerves: Infusion as basil.

MINT:
Hiccoughs; indigestion: Chew mint (peppermint) leaves to cure hiccoughs. Mint tea (see Teas) for indigestion.

PARSLEY:
Anaemia; for skin. For anaemia eat as much raw parsley as possible. For the skin make an infusion with 15 ml (3 teasp) fresh or 5 ml (1 teasp) dried per 600 ml (1 pt) boiling water.

ROSEMARY
Menstrual pains; tenseness: Make an infusion with 30 g (1 oz) fresh young tops and leaves or 15 g (½ oz) dried, per 600 ml (1 pt) boiling water. One teacup daily.

SAGE:
Headaches; catarrh; soothing nerves: Sage tea (see Teas) for headaches. With honey for catarrh and to calm nerves. A mild sage tea, cooled, applied externally for sunburn.

SORREL:
Swelling from fall: Crush leaves and apply to injury or crush leaves and dab on juice.

THYME:
Bad breath; headaches: Infusion as basil.

INDEX